Your Promised Life

Daily Devotions
Based on Promises of God

Kay Bryant

Endorsement #1

The Bible can be intimidating for all Christians. I love how this 26-week Bible study encourages and motivates its readers to daily get into the book that "just keeps giving" the Bible. It is so crucial for Christians to take time EVERYDAY to get into the word and strengthen their personal relationship with God. This study is perfect for all believers who want to take their faith to an entirely different level. Learn how to study the Bible daily, memorize scripture, discover your life purpose, and life verse. These are tools I use daily to prepare for the battles that I face daily, I highly recommend and challenge you to take that next step in your faith.
– *Dr. Deborah Ormonde, Author, Speaker, President & Founder of Be Finally Free.*

Endorsement #2

In her work, Promised Life, Kay Bryant establishes the value of memorizing portions of the Bible. She recognizes that we need to be incentivized to want to commit God's Word to memory. To accomplish that, she looks to the Bible itself to inspire us to memorize key verses.

Once the reader apprehends why it's highly beneficial to memorize biblical passages, with laser focus, Kay zeros in on how to commit the Scripture to memory. To practically help the reader memorize a specific verse, Kay goes beyond rote memorization techniques. She recognizes the importance of heightening the reader's understanding of a text. How does Kay achieve this? Well, she does what any competent educator does. As an experienced teacher of adults and children, Kay takes the time to provide the background and context of verse that is to be memorized. Additionally, she explains portions of the memory verse and abundantly incorporates relevant cross references, personal experiences, quotes, and songs. Additionally, she will help the reader comprehend key phrases that need to be understood. When it is necessary, Kay also expounds upon essential words from a memory verse through the lens of several different theological angles.

No doubt, she would probably say that comprehension is key to memorization. Fortunately, rather than the reader needing to unpack the meanings of various Bible verses, Kay does this for the Bible student. It's like she fast tracks a person to the worthwhile goal of learning and owning the Good Book!

For each day, Kay provides an easy to accomplish assignment for the memorizer. This section jumps out to the reader with the words "To Do". In these sections, Kay suggests what to read, memorize, and review.

To lighten the mood, she offers a "Smile for the day," a playful one-liner that keeps us engaged. Kay would concur with the ol' endearing lyric, "Just a spoonful of sugar helps the medicine go down in a most delightful way" from the movie, Mary Poppins.

The goal of Kay's book is to get the reader to fall in love with Holy Writ by studying and memorizing its truths. If the reader takes up Kay on her challenge, then he/she will have learned 26 weeks worth of wonderful verses from the Word of God. Now THERE'S a challenge worth taking! Are you up for it? Only you can answer that question.

On a personal note, I have had the distinct privilege of being Kay's pastor for well over a decade. In addition to being a dear friend and sister in the Lord, Kay is well-respected by everyone in our church as a truly devoted woman of God, who creatively teaches the Word of God in our women's ministry. By reading and applying this refreshing book to your life, you will be positively impacted for time and eternity!

Devoted to the One Who Calms Storms, Moves Mountains & Changes Lives,

Jeff Kaplan
Senior Pastor
Shepherd of the Hills

Endorsement #3

I have LOVED reading through this devotional you wrote. What a great piece of work the Lord has done through you. Each day was filled with scripture, truth and insight and practical suggestions on how to actually live out the truth mentioned. I thought they were very well done as far as what was included, the length of each day's devo was about perfect and it wasn't filled with your words of encouragement only, but with God's Word which is ultimately what restores the soul.

Thank you for allowing me to read them and I hope the endorsement was enough to convey how special this work is.

Love you my friend,
Teri Thompson
Founder Kern County Christian Women's Conference

TABLE OF CONTENTS

MY PROMISED LIFE

God's "divine power has granted to us everything pertaining to
life and godliness, through
the true knowledge of Him who called us by His own glory and
excellence. For by
these He has granted to us His precious and magnificent promises, so that by them
you may become partakers of the divine nature, having escaped
the corruption that
is in the world by lust." (2 Peter 1:3-4)

MY PROMISED LIFE

God's "divine power has granted to us everything pertaining to
life and godliness, through
the true knowledge of Him who called us by His own glory and
excellence. For by
these He has granted to us His precious and magnificent promises, so that by them
you may become partakers of the divine nature, having escaped
the corruption that
is in the world by lust." (2 Peter 1:3-4)

INTRODUCTION

The Bible offers wondrous insights into living the Christian life daily. Regardless of how many times you read a passage or chapter in the Bible, something new will invariably claim your attention.

The Bible is the book that "just keeps giving." So, read the Bible daily and accept God's words daily as the words for that particular day. Don't read the Bible like a novel. Read the Bible daily like you're preparing for a test. Here is a daily guide for the chapter/chapters you read. Do all or pick one to do for each day.

A Daily Guide for Reading
1. What is the topic of today's reading?
2. Are there any promises in today's reading?
3. What is this passage saying to me?
4. Was there a command given?
5. Is there an action step for me to take today?
6. Is there a thought or verse to think about throughout the day?

Your Study and Meditation - You might want to record your thoughts in a journal.

<u>Your Life Purpose</u>

In a front page in your Bible write your heartfelt prayer for your life to God. This is the life you'd like to live through Him. Here is what I wrote for me.:

"My <u>life purpose</u> is to live the plan You have for my life to the fullest, to daily pray for and listen for Your guiding hand, to let Your light shine through my life so that I can leave a legacy of faith for my children and grandchildren."

"<u>My dream</u> is to bring more laughter into the world and to remember that only through Your power can my purpose and my dream become my reality."

"I want to be a "sparkler" for You"

<u>Your lifetime verse</u> – If you have a favorite verse, like your "go-to"verse, write it down
Mine is James 4:8 - "draw near to God and He will draw near to you"

Why Memorize Scripture?

Ephesians 6 talks about putting on the armor of God. Verse 11 says, "put on the full armor of God so that you will be able to stand firm against the schemes of the devil." Just like a warrior in biblical times put on his full armor every time he went into battle, so we too must put on the full armor every day to go to battle against the devil. The only piece of armor that's used to attack is the sword. Put on the sword of the Spirit, which is the Word of God. So, you're on a battle field and how will you be able to use the sword of the Spirit in battle if you haven't memorized verses to draw from? You're helpless. You have nothing to fight with.

Pastor Rick Warren says, " if you're serious about being spiritually strong and mature, the greatest habit you can develop is memorizing scripture. Memorizing scripture helps you have victory over worry, keeps you encouraged, and develops your prayer life."

What else does the Bible say about memorizing scripture? What other benefits are there for you when you memorize scriptures?

1. We already know memorizing scripture is a <u>powerful weapon against spiritual attacks. (Ephesians 6: 13-17)</u>

2. When God's Word is in your heart, the Holy Spirit causes it to burst forth in your mind as a protectant against sin. (Psalm 119:11)
3. When you treasure scripture in your heart, it resounds in your mind; (Luke 2:19.51)
4. Memorizing scripture encourages us to do God's will. (Psalm 40:8)
5. Memorized scripture is a guide for our walk with the Lord: guides our steps (Psalm 11)
6. Memorizing scripture will benefit your life. "Rmember what Christ taught, and let His words enrich your lives and make you wise." (Colossians 3:16)

Why memorize promises?

1. Memorizing promises teaches us God's truth. (Proverbs 3:3-4)
2. Memorizing promises helps us grow in our trust of God & faith in Him by renewing our mind. (2 Corinthians 4:16)
3. Memorizing scripture reminds us that we are partakers of the divine nature (2 Peter 1:3-4)
4. Memorizing scripture helps us to dwell on "PLANTR" – Phillippians 4:8 the things we are to dwell on: Pure, Lovely, Admirable, Noble, True, Right

Memorizing a verse each day
Just might help me along the way.
And when God says "I WILL" to me
That's a blessing I must see.
Say the verse again and again.
When it's memorized say, "amen."
Add a memory verse each week
And my faith will start to peak.

Weekly Format

Each week, we will focus on one verse to memorize. Each daily devotional will elaborate on the main idea of the memory verse for that week. At the end of 26 weeks, you will have memorized 26 of God's promises to you.

At the end of each week are 2 pages for you to record thoughts, prayer requests and things you are thankful for

Also included: A "laugh for the day." I'm a big believer in laughter as a medicine for well being.

Week 1 Day 1 <u>Memory verse:</u> "as for me I WILL call upon the name of the Lord and the Lord SHALL save me." Psalm 55:16

POWER

You'll know if a Bible verse is a promise when you read the words WILL and/or SHALL When God is making a promise the Bible verse clearly states I will, God will or the Lord will. As you look through the alphabetized Promise list this becomes evident.

So what does "call upon the name of the Lord" mean? In Psalm 54:1, David says, "save me, O God, by Your name and vindicate me by Your power." When David calls upon the name of the Lord, he's recognizing the full power God has just in His name. So, one meaning of "call upon the Lord" is a prayer for God's power to help you. It's saying to God, "I trust You, have faith in You and recognize that even in Your name there is the power to save me and help me." Throughout the Psalms David repeatedly gives glory to God. Again, in Psalm 124:8 David says, "our help is in the name of the Lord who made heaven and earth." Have you ever prayed, "save me O God, by Your name?"

This power in His name reminds me of one of my favorite hymns: "Jesus, Jesus, Jesus. There's just something about that name. Master, Savior, Jesus, like the fragrance after the rain. Jesus, Jesus, Jesus, let all heaven and earth proclaim. Kings and kingdoms will all pass away but there's something about that name."

To Do: Read Psalm 55
Repeat the memory verse several times throughout the day

Smile for the day: How does Moses make his tea? Hebrews it

KAY BRYANT

Week 1 Day 2 <u>Memory verse</u>: "as for me I WILL call upon the name of the Lord and the Lord SHALL save me." Psalm 55:16

ACKNOWLEDGMENT

At least 51 times in the Bible the phrase "call upon the name of the Lord" is used. Most of these appear in the books of Acts and Romans. One of the first is in Genesis 12. Here the Lord appeared to Abram (before changing his name to Abraham) and led him, his wife Sarai and his nephew Lot to Canaan. Abram was 75 years old at the time. (verse 5) And, the Lord said to him, "to your descendants I will give this land" (verse 7) Abram went to a nearby mountain top and built an altar and <u>called upon the name of the Lord.</u> (verse 8) In Genesis 21:33, Abram, now Abraham was at Beersheba and planted a Tamarisk tree and <u>called upon the name of the Lord.</u> Psalm 18:3 says, "I will call upon the Lord who is worthy to be praised."

In both of these circumstances, Abraham is acknowledging God for His provision. It is referring to saying a prayer. Sarah Young in her book, Jesus Calling, says when you want to feel the presence of Jesus say "Jesus" out loud. It works. I find myself doing it a lot when I'm driving or in the midst of a busy, non-stop day or just because I instantly want to acknowledge His presence in my life.

To Do: Read Psalm 18
       Repeat the memory verse several times today throughout the day

Smile for the day: The good Lord didn't create anything without a purpose, but mosquitos come close.

Week 1 Day 3 <u>Memory verse:</u> " as for me I WILL call upon the name of the Lord and the Lord SHALL save me." Psalm 55:16

<u>REPENTANCE</u>

Another meaning for "call upon the name of the Lord" is repentance. Repentance, in the Bible, refers to a change of mind resulting in a change of action. It's choosing to turn aside from sinful ways and turn to God. Joel was an Old Testament prophet who warned, in detail, about the coming Day of the Lord which refers to end times. Joel 2:32 says, "and it will come about that whoever calls upon the name of the Lord will be delivered." You will be delivered, forgiven of your sins, past, present and future. It's never too late as long as you're living. God desires for all people to repent and turn to Him. For this reason, He is waiting for as many people as possible to make that decision.

The words of one of my favorite hymns is: Turn Your Eyes Upon Jesus. Look full in his wonderful face. And the things of earth will grow strangely dim in the light of His glory and grace."

To Do: Read Joel 2

Repeat the memory verse several times throughout the day

Smile for the day: If God is your co-pilot, swap seats.

Week 1 Day 4 <u>Memory verse:</u> "as for me I WILL call upon the name of the Lord and the Lord SHALL save me." Psalm 55:16

<u>SALVATION</u>

Romans 10:9 says, "that if you confess with your mouth Jesus as Lord, and believe in your heart that God raised Him from the dead, you will be saved." And, Romans 10:13 says, "whoever will call upon the name of the Lord will be saved." Salvation is for everyone. Romans 10:11 goes on to say that "whoever believes in Him will not be disappointed." Salvation is delieverance from sin and its' consequences.

When you "call upon the name of the Lord" it is a prayer. And, this brings to mind one of my favorite hymns: Love Lifted Me. The words to this hymn are: "I was sinking deep in sin, far from the peaceful shore, very deeply stained within, sinking to rise no more; but the Master of that sea heard my despairing cry, from the waters lifted me – now safe am I. Love lifted me. Love lifted me. When nothing else could help, love lifted me."

To Do: Read Romans 10
  Repeat the memory verse several times throughout the day

Smile for the day: When you get to your wit's end, you'll find God lives there.

Week 1 Day 5 <u>Memory verse:</u> "As for me I WILL call upon the name of the Lord and the Lord SHALL save me." Psalm 55:16

DISTRESS

Another meaning for "call upon the name of the Lord" is when in distress. In Psalm 118:5, David says, "from my distress I called upon the Lord. The Lord answered me and set me in a large place." The text says "if the Lord is for you, you need not fear." (verse 6) And, goes on to say "it's better to take refuge in the Lord than trust in man." (verse 8) I picture a large place as a safe place, a place where I'm protected and loved. And, it's large because I'm at peace – full of peace.

So, this week we've seen to "call upon the name of the Lord" is a prayer and we've seen some biblical people who did this for various reasons: recognizing the power in Jesus name, acknowledging God's provision, asking for forgiveness/repentance, praying for salvation and praying when you're distressed.

This reminds me of the hymn I Will Call Upon The Lord. "I will call upon the Lord who is worthy to be praised. So shall I be saved from my enemies. I will call upon the Lord. The Lord liveth and blessed be the rock, and let the God of my salvation be exalted"

To Do: Read Psalm 118

Repeat this memory verse several times throughout the day

Smile for the day: Forbidden fruits create many jams.

Week 1 Day 6 Review your memory verse. Record thoughts from this week's devotions and / or prayer requests.

_____

_____

_____

_____

_____

_____

_____

_____

_____

_____

_____

_____

_____

_____

_____

_____

_____

_____

_____

_____

_____

_____

_____

_____

_____

_____

_____

_____

_____

Week 1 Day 7 Review your memory verse. When we pray our prayers should include thanksgiving. Record here what you are thankful for today. Philippians 4:6 "Be anxious for nothing, but in everything by prayer and supplication with thanksgiving let your requests be made known to God."

_____

_____

_____

_____

_____

_____

_____

_____

_____

_____

_____

_____

_____

_____

_____

_____

_____

_____

_____

_____

_____

_____

Week 2 Day 1 <u>Memory verse:</u> "But the Lord is faithful and WILL strengthen and protect you from the evil one." II Thessalonians 3:3

FAITHFUL

What does faithful mean? It means steadfast in keeping promises. We are reassured of this promise in Matthew 28:20 when the Lord reinforces his steadfastness: "And be sure of this, that I am with you always, even to the end of the world." So, put your belief and trust in and loyalty to God because He is faithful. In this memory verse, Paul is encouraging the new believers in the church of Thessalonica as their persecution for their faith has not subsided. Paul prays that the Lord will direct their paths into the love of God.

I Corinthians 10:13 offers us comfort and assurance: "No temptation has overtaken you but such as is common to man; and God is faithful, who will not allow you to be tempted beyond what you are able, but will provide the way of escape also, so that you'll be able to endure it."

To Do: Read II Thessalonians 3
Repeat the memory verse several times today & repeat the 1st weeks memory verse

Smile for the day: We don't change the message. The message changes us.

Week 2 Day 2 <u>Memory verse:</u> "But the Lord is faithful and WILL strengthen and protect you from the evil one." II Thessalonians 3:3

PROTECT

The Lord repeatedly tells us in the Bible that He will protect us. But, we have to choose to believe it. God says in Ecclesiastes 7:12, "For wisdom is protection just as money is protection, but the advantage of knowledge is that wisdom preserves the lives of its possessors." That's quite a promise in itself. Protect means to guard or shield. I Peter 1:5 assures us "we are protected by the power of God through faith for a salvation ready to be revealed in the last time." Protection is a very comforting word. Think about times throughout your life when you felt protected. God's desire is for you to feel protected.

Psalm 91 is a chapter about how comforted we can feel dwelling in the shelter of the Most High. God promises in verse 11 "to guard you in all your ways." And, in verse 15, He promises "I will be with him in trouble." I John 5:18 says, "He who was born of God keeps him; and the evil one does not touch him."

To Do: Read Psalm 91

Repeat the memory verse several times today & repeat the 1st weeks memory verse

Smile for the day: We were called to be witnesses, not lawyers or judges

Week 2 Day 3 <u>Memory verse</u>: "but the Lord is faithful and WILL strengthen and protect you from the evil one." II Thessalonians 3:3

<u>QUOTING SCRIPTURE</u>

Jesus fasted 40 days and 40 nights in the wilderness. He then became hungry. Satan came and tempted Him 3 times. All 3 times Jesus quoted scripture and then Satan departed. Here we have a perfect example of the power of the Word to use against the evil one. And, since all God's promises are true, you know you're using the "sword of the spirit" - which is the true word of God. This is your weapon.

One of the first bible verses you memorized was probably The Lord's Prayer. This is referred to in Luke 11:2-4 as the Model Prayer, meaning a prayer guide for teaching a new Christian how to pray.

I personalized this prayer to make it more meaningful for me. So pray for strength and protection.

Our Father in heaven
Hallowed be your name.
Your kingdom come
Your will be done
On earth as it is in heaven
Give me this day my daily bread,
And forgive me my sins
For I also forgive everyone
who is indebted to me
And do not lead me into temptation
but deliver me from the <u>evil one.</u>

To Do: Read Luke 11
Repeat the memory verse several times today & repeat the 1ˢᵗ weeks memory verse.

Smile for the day: Quit griping about your church; if it was perfect, you couldn't belong

<u>TRUST</u>

David speaks a lot in the book of Psalms about the Lord's protection. In doing so, he shows his complete trust and faith in the Lord and His protection. Perhaps David's daily motto was "The Lord is my strength and my shield. My heart trusts in Him and I am helped." (Psalm 28:7) Until you have this same trust in your heart, this might be a good verse to repeat daily. Here are some other examples found in Psalms.

Psalm 112:1 talks about "how blessed is the man who fears the Lord, who greatly delights in His commandments." And in verse 7, "he will not fear evil tidings; his heart is steadfast, trusting in the Lord." When we choose to live by faith, trust becomes easier for us. We also must choose to fear (revere) the Lord to feel peace about His protecting us. Psalm 91:11 says, "For He will give His angels charge concerning you, to guard you in all your ways." There's a promise worth holding on to. Read the Word, believe and trust in what God says He will do. Psalm 56:4 says, " In God, whose word I praise, in God I have put my trust; I shall not be afraid." That's a promise you're making to yourself because you trust in God and His word.

To Do: Read Psalm 56

Repeat the memory verse several times today & repeat the 1st weeks memory verse

Smile for the day: God doesn't call the qualified, He qualifies the called

Week 2 Day 5 <u>Memory verse:</u> "but the Lord is faithful and WILL strengthen and protect you from the evil one." II Thessalonians 3:3

<u>EVIL ONE</u>

Who is the evil one? The evil one is a demon, fallen angel, also referred to as the devil and satan. In John 8:44 Jesus is talking to the scribes and Pharisees and He says, " You are of your father the devil, and you want to do the desires of your father. He was a murderer from the beginning, and does not stand in the truth because there is no truth in him. Whenever he speaks a lie, he speaks from his own nature, for he is a liar and the father of lies." I John 3:8 says, "the one who practices sin is of the devil; for the devil has sinned from the beginning. The Son of God appeared for this reason, to destroy the works of the devil."

In Acts 13:10, Paul is speaking to a magician and says, " You are full of deceit and fraud, you son of the devil, you enemy of righteousness." So, the evil one is (1) a murderer, (2) has no truth, (3) the father of lies, (4) sinned from the beginning (remember Eve in the Garden of Eden), (5) enemy of righteousness. His goal is to cause you to lose trust and faith and hope in the Lord.

To Do: Read I John 3
Repeat the memory verse several times today & repeat the 1st weeks memory verse

Smile for the day: The task ahead of us is never as great as the power behind us.

Week 2 Day 6 Review your memory verse. Record thoughts from this week's devotions and / or prayer requests.

_____

_____

_____

_____

_____

_____

_____

_____

_____

_____

_____

_____

_____

_____

_____

_____

_____

_____

_____

_____

_____

_____

_____

_____

_____

_____

Week 2 Day 7 Review your memory verse. When we pray our prayers should include thanksgiving. Record here what you are thankful for today. Philippians 4:6 "Be anxious for nothing, but in everything by prayer and supplication with thanksgiving let your requests be made known to God."

_____

_____

_____

_____

_____

_____

_____

_____

_____

_____

_____

_____

_____

_____

_____

_____

_____

_____

_____

_____

_____

_____

_____

_____

_____

_____

Week 3 Day 1 <u>Memory verse:</u> "Call to me and I WILL answer you and I WILL show you great things which you do not know." Jeremiah 33:3

PROPHECY

In the Old Testament God spoke to the prophets directly and that is how God's wisdom was given to the Israelites. Jeremiah was a prophet during the reign of King Josiah, the reign of his son Jehoiakim followed by the reign of Josiah's son Zedekiah. It's interesting to note there was a 30 year period when God didn't speak. This was the period of time between the prophets Isaiah and Jeremiah when the Israelites had turned away from God. In Jeremiah 33 God is telling Jeremiah His plans to rebuild Judah. God goes into detail how He will restore Judah and Jerusalem. It is a prophecy. The word prophecy means to speak forth the mind and counsel of God.

Through Jeremiah the prophet, the people were shown great things which they did not know. Here are a few of God's promises in Jeremiah 33: "I WILL cleanse them from all of their iniquity."(verse 8) "I WILL restore the fortunes of Judah and Israel." (verse 7) "I WILL reveal to them an abundance of peace and truth." (verse 6) "I WILL heal them." (verse 6) "I WILL fulfill the good word which I have spoken concerning the house of Israel and the house of Judah." (verse 14)

To Do: Read Jeremiah 33
Repeat the memory verse several times today & repeat the first 2 weeks memory verses

Smile for the day: A lot of church members who are singing "Standing on the Promises" are sitting on the premise

Week 3 Day 2 <u>Memory verse:</u> "Call to me and I WILL answer you and I WILL show you great things which you do not know." Jeremiah 33:3

WISDOM

A proverb is a short saying or story which gives insight on life and human behavior. Proverbs is full of wise and timeless messages that reflect so much wisdom and insights into daily living – learning great things. King Solomon was wiser than any man before or after him. He also spoke 3000 proverbs. In Proverbs 3, Solomon says what wisdom is. Here are just a few insights: Wisdom's profit is better than the profit of silver; (verse 14) wisdom is life to your soul; (verse 22) wisdom is more precious than jewels; (verse 15) wisdom is a tree of life. (verse 18)

Wisdom is personified in Chapter 8. Verse 6 says, "Listen for I, wisdom, will speak noble things and the opening of my lips will reveal right things." "All the utterances of my mouth are in righeousness."(verse 8) "Counsel is mine and sound wisdom; I am understanding, power is mine." (verse 12) Take time to meditate on the proverbs and perhaps write notes in the margins and pick out the main thoughts you want to remember.

To Do: Read Proverbs 8

　　　Repeat the memory verse several times today & repeat the first 2 weeks memory verses

Smile for the day: God grades on the cross, not the curve

Week 3 Day 3 <u>Memory verse:</u> "Call to Me and I WILL answer you and I WILL show you great things which you do not know." Jeremiah 33:3

ANSWERS

Who are some people in the Bible that called to God and He answered? He answered Jonah when he was in the stomach of the fish. Jonah 2:2 says, " I called out of my distress to the Lord, and He answered me. I cried for help from the depth of Sheol; You heard my voice." And, in Jonah 2:10, God answered his prayer: "Then the Lord commanded the fish, and it vomited Jonah up onto the dry land." And, Jonah was thankful (verse 9) and learned some great things that day. David says in Psalm 3:4, "I was crying to the Lord with my voice, and He answered me from His holy mountain." Samuel, speaking to Israel in I Samuel 12:17,18 says, " Is it not the wheat harvest today? I will call to the Lord, that He may send thunder and rain. Then you will know and see that your wickedness is great which you have done in the sight of the Lord by asking for yourselves a king. So Samuel called to the Lord, and the Lord sent thunder and rain that day: and all the people greatly feared the Lord and Samuel."

To do: Read Jonah 2

Repeat the memory verse several times today & repeat the first 2 weeks memory verses

Smile for the day: Don't put a question mark where God puts a period.

KAY BRYANT

Week 3 Day 4 <u>Memory verse:</u> "Call to me and I WILL answer you and I WILL show you great things which you do not know." Jeremiah 33:3

<u>CALL</u>

Many people call upon the Lord when they are in trouble. Some people only call upon the name of the Lord when in trouble. Psalm 50:15 says, "Call upon Me in the day of trouble; I shall rescue you, and you will honor Me." This implies that we have a thankful spirit when God rescues us from trouble.

Psalm 107:6 says, Then they cried out to the Lord in their trouble; He delivered them out of their distresses." And, verse 8 says, "Let them give thanks to the Lord for His lovingkindness." These two thoughts are repeated three more times in Psalm 107.

And, the promise for the Christian in Psalm 91:4 says, "he will call upon Me, and I will answer him; I will be with him in trouble; I will rescue him and honor him." And another promise follows in verse 16: "With a long life I will satisfy him and let him see My salvation." When we don't get the answer we want, we think God hasn't listened and responded. But, His promise, when we call upon His name in trouble, is that He will hear us and be with us.

To Do: Read Psalm 107
    Repeat the memory verse several times today & repeat the first 2 weeks memory verses

Smile for the day: God promises a safe landing, not a calm passage.

Week 3 Day 5 <u>Memory verse:</u> "Call to me and I WILL answer you and I WILL show you great things which you do not know." Jeremiah 33:3

<u>KNOWLEDGE</u>

Remember from our introudction that the Bible is the book that just keeps on giving. God shows us great things through the lives and expereiences of people throughout the Bible. God is the God of knowledge. II Peter 1:2,3 says, "Grace and peace be multiplied to you in the knowledge of God and of Jesus our Lord; seeing that His divine power has granted to us everything pertaining to life and godlinesss, through the true knowledge of Him who called us by His own glory and excellence."

God does not only show us great things for our benefit. He also show us great things that will not benefit us. Here are some words of knowledge, that Solomon shares in Proverbs 23. These are called the "Do Nots:" "DO NOT weary yourself to gain wealth." (verse 4) "DO NOT eat the bread of a selfish man." (verse 6) "DO NOT speak in the hearing of a fool." (verse 9) "DO NOT hold back discipline from the child." (verse 13) "DO NOT let your heart envy sinners." (verse 17) You want to find out great things which you do not know, read the book of Proverbs and definitely take notes. Proverbs has 31 chapters. Whatever your Bible reading is each day, add a chapter of Proverbs each day. You will definitely learn great things and grow in wisdom.

To Do: Read II Peter 2

Repeat the memory verse several times today & repeat the first 2 weeks memory verses

Smile for the day: Opportunity may knock once, but temptation bangs on your front door forever

KAY BRYANT

Week 3 Day 6 Review your memory verse. Record thoughts from this week's devotions and / or prayer requests.

_____
_____
_____
_____
_____
_____
_____
_____
_____
_____
_____
_____
_____
_____
_____
_____
_____
_____
_____
_____
_____
_____
_____
_____
_____
_____
_____
_____
_____
_____
_____

Week 3 Day 7 Review your memory verse. When we pray our prayers should include thanksgiving. Record here what you are thankful for today. Philippians 4:6 "Be anxious for nothing, but in everything by prayer and supplication with thanksgiving let your requests be made known to God."

_____
_____
_____
_____
_____
_____
_____
_____
_____
_____
_____
_____
_____
_____
_____
_____
_____
_____
_____
_____
_____
_____
_____

Week 4 Day 1 <u>Memory verse:</u> "Draw near to God and He WILL draw near to you." James 4:8

SUBMIT

In James 4, James, the brother of Jesus, talks about the source of conflicts and quarrels among us. He defines that source as pleasures that rage within us and refers to lust, murder, envy and asking God with wrong motives. (verses 1-3) In summary of these thoughts, he says in verse 4, "Therefore whoever wishes to be a friend of the world makes himself an enemy of God." His conclusion to these thoughts is "submit to God. Resist the devil and he will flee." The point of all of this is our memory verse, "Draw near to God and He will draw near to you."

I have a favorite hymn that helps me visualize being near to God. It's called "In The Garden"

I come to the garden alone,
And He walks with me, and He talks with me

While the dew is still on the roses;
And He tells me I am His own,

And the voice I hear, falling on my ear,
And the joy we share as we tarry there,

The Son of God discloses
None other has ever known.

To Do: Read James 4
> Repeat the memory verse several times today & repeat the first 3 weeks memory verses

Smile for the day: Peace starts with a smile

<u>SEEK</u>

Read II Chronicles to find numeous life lessons and truths, all of which will help you on your path to holiness. In II Chronicles 15:2, the Spirit of God comes on the prophet Azariah and he says to King Asa and all of Judah and Benjamin, "the Lord is with you when you are with Him. And, if you seek Him, He will let you find Him." King Asa took courage from these words and removed all the abominable idols and led the people back to the Lord. He was a good King. And, verse 4 says, "but in their distress they turned to the Lord God of Israel, and they sought Him, and He let them find Him."

Zechariah 1:3 says, "Return to Me, declares the Lord of Hosts, that I may return to you." When we don't draw near to God, we can't feel His presence or His nearness. We must want to seek His nearness.

To Do: Read II Chronicles 15

Repeat the memory verse several times today & repeat the first 3 week memory verses

Smile for the day: God is like Bayer aspirin, He works miracles

Week 4 Day 3 <u>Memory verse:</u> "Draw near to God and He WILL draw near to you." James 4:8

MUSIC

One way to draw near to God is by singing hymns. One of the blessings I enjoy is playing the piano and singing hymns. I always feel God's presence. David is the perfect example to follow when it comes to singing to the Lord. Many verses in the Psalms start with "sing to Him a new song." Here is Psalm 33:1-3 which I titled "Shout For Joy:" "Sing for joy in the Lord, O you righteous ones; praise is becoming to the upright. Give thanks to the Lord with the lyre (a stringed musical instrument that is plucked). Sing praises to Him with a harp of ten strings. Sing to Him a new song; play skillfully with a shout of joy." So, sing to the Lord is (1) a way to express joy to the Lord.

Psalm 147:7 says, "Sing to the Lord with thanksgiving." So, sing to the Lord is (2) a way of showing thanksgiving. Psalm 147:1 says, "Sing praises to the Lord for it is good to sing praises to our God; for it is pleasant and praise is becoming." So, sing to the Lord is (3) a pleasant way to praise God.

In I Chronicles 16, David offers a song of praise when the ark of the covenant came to the city of David. In verses 8-11, he says, "Oh give thanks to the Lord, call upon His name; make known His deeds among the peoples. Sing to Him, sing praise to Him; speak of all his wonders. Glory in His name; let the heart of those who seek the Lord be glad." Follow David's example in drawing near.

To Do: Read Psalm 33

> Repeat the memory verse several times today & repeat the first 3 weeks memory verses

Smile for the day: God is like coke. He's the real thing

Week 4 Day 4 <u>Memory verse:</u> "Draw near to God & He WILL draw near to you."

FEAR OF THE LORD

"Therefore, He (Jesus) is able to save forever those who draw near to God through Him, since He always lives to make intercession for them." (Hebrews 7:25) Wow. This verse makes me think of the importance of "the fear of the Lord." This fear is a reverential awe where we revere His power and glory. This means when we have a fear of the Lord, we are acknowledging His steadfast love and faithfulness. Here are some verses addressing the "fear of the Lord:"

Proverbs 19:23 - "The fear of the Lord leads to life, so that one may sleep satisfied, untouched by evil."

Psalm 34:9 - " O fear the Lord, you His saints; For to those who fear Him there is no want"

Psalm 111:10 says, "the fear of the Lord is the beginning of wisdom; a good understanding have all those who do His commandments; His praise endures forever."

To Do: Read Psalm 111
Repeat the memory verse several times today & repeat the first 3 weeks memory verses

Smile for the day: God is like Hallmark cards, He cares enough to send His very best

KAY BRYANT

Week 4 Day 5 <u>Memory verse:</u> "Draw near to God and He WILL draw near to you." James 4:8

<u>A PLAN</u>

This week we've seen the things to do to draw near to God:

(1) Submit to God. Yield to God's power. Surrender your dreams, plans, goals to Him

(2) Seek God earnestly. Seek His righteousness and He will be near to you

(3) Sing to the Lord a new song. Through hymns of praise and worship, we draw near to God

(4) Revere the Lord for His power and glory, knowing that the fear (awe) of the Lord is the beginning of wisdom.

So, how do we do all these things? You do it through prayer, reading and studying the Bible, inspirational reading of other books, being a part of a Bible Study, through the preaching of pastors.

First, you need to have a strong desire to draw near to God and to get to know Him better. The closer you become to God, the more blessed you will be.

To Do: Write out on the following page your plan on how you will draw near to God. Review any scripture passages that were very meaningful to you and pull out your gems of wisdom.

Repeat the memory verse several times today & repeat the first 3 weeks memory verses.

Smile for the day: PHARMACIST: A helper on the farm

Week 4 Day 6 Review your memory verse. Record thoughts from this week's devotions and / or prayer requests.

_____

_____

_____

_____

_____

_____

_____

_____

_____

_____

_____

_____

_____

_____

_____

_____

_____

_____

_____

_____

_____

_____

_____

_____

_____

_____

Week 4 Day 7 Review your memory verse. When we pray our prayers should include thanksgiving. Record here what you are thankful for today. Philippians 4:6 "Be anxious for nothing, but in everything by prayer and supplication with thanksgiving let your requests be made known to God."

_____

_____

_____

_____

_____

_____

_____

_____

_____

_____

_____

_____

_____

_____

_____

_____

_____

_____

_____

_____

_____

_____

_____

_____

_____

Week 5 Day 1 <u>Memory verse:</u> "Everyone who confesses Me before men, I WILL also confess him before my Father." Matthew 10:32

<u>CONFESS</u>

To confess is to acknowledge and admit your sins to God. In Matthew 10, Jesus gives instructions to His disciples. He gives His disciples authority over unclean spirits, to cast them out and to heal every kind of disease and sickness. And, Jesus goes into detail to encourage them when they are speaking (confessing) about Him to others. He assures them not to worry about what they will say for the Spirit of God speaks in them. By the way, as disciples in today's world, we have this same confidence when sharing the gosepl: the Spirit of God will guide us.

He assures the disciples that they are more valuable than small sparrows who are not forgotten by God. And, He tells them the very hairs of their heads are all numbered. (verses 29-31) These are the verses leading up to today's memory verse. The promise verse today is one they can hold on to for themselves, and share with those they are ministering to, with full confidence.

To do: Read Matthew 10
Repeat the memory verse several times today & repeat the first 4 weeks memory verses

Smile for the day: God is like Walmart. He has everything

KAY BRYANT

Week 5 Day 2 <u>Memory verse:</u> "Everyone who confesses me before men, I WILL also confess him before My Father." Matthew 10:32

<u>BAPTISM</u>

There are many references in the New Testament about a new believer confessing before men. This usually was a part of the baptism. In Matthew 28:19, Jesus is speaking to His disciples and says, "Go therefore and make disciples of all nations, baptizing them in the name of the Father and the Son and the Holy Spirit." And, Mark 16:16 says, "He who has believed and has been baptized shall be saved; but he who has disbelieved shall be condemned."

What are the reasons to be baptized in addition to what we have read here? Jesus was baptized to fulfill God. It was a righteous requirement. (Matthew 3:15) Galations 3:27 says, "for all of you who were baptized into Christ have clothed yourselves with Christ." And, again, in I Corinthians 12:13a, "For by one Spirit we were all baptized into one body."

The reasons to be baptized as a public confession before men: (1) we fulfill the righteous requirement which Christ did when He was baptized; (2) submersion in the water signifies the end of the old way of living and a new start; (3) when baptized you become a member of the body of Christ. So, being baptized is a public confession which is an integral part of becoming a new believer.

To do: Read Matthew 3
Repeat the memory verse several times today & repeat the first 4 weeks memory verses.

Smile for the day: God is like Allstate. You're in good hands with Him.

Week 5 Day 3 <u>Memory verse:</u> "Everyone who shall confess Me before men, I WILL also confess him before My Father." Matthew 10:32

THE ANGELS

Not only will Jesus confess to His Father everyone who confesses Him to men, He will also confess him before the angels of God. (Luke 12:8) Why does He do this? Because, "there is great joy in the presence of the angels of God over one sinner who repents." (Luke 15:10).

Jesus says in Luke 15:7, "I tell you that there will be more joy in heaven over one sinner who repents than over ninety-nine righteous persons who need no repentance." Jesus goes on to make this point with the parable of The Prodigal Son. (Luke 15) The father had compassion on his son when he returned and organized a big celebration and said, "this son of mine was dead and has come to life again; he was lost and has been found."(verse 24)

Wow! Wouldn't you want to see the angels in their moments of joy?

To do: Read Luke 15

Repeat the memory verse several times today & repeat the first 4 weeks memory verses

Smile for the day: God is like hair spray. He holds through all kinds of weather

KAY BRYANT

Week 5 Day 4 <u>Memory verse:</u> "Everyone who shall confess Me before men, I WILL also confess him before My Father." Matthew 10:32

<u>OVERCOMER</u>

Revelations 3:5 adds to the fact that Jesus will confess him before His Father, by adding that the person who overcomes "will be clothed in white garments; and I (Jesus) will not erase his name from the book of life." An overcomer is one who resists sin. Romans 12:21 says, "do not be overcome by evil, but overcome evil with good."

Another promise is made In Revelation 2:7, "to him who overcomes, I will grant to eat of the tree of life which is in the paradise of God." What is this tree of life? In Revelation 22:1-2, the disciple John says, "then He showed me a river of the water of life coming from the throne of God and on either side of the river was the tree of life. It was bearing 12 kinds of fruit, yielding it's fruit every month and the leaves were for the healing of the nations." Solomon in three different places in Proverbs says these three things about a tree of life (remember this is before Jesus): wisdom is like a tree of life. (Proverbs 3:18) Desire fulfilled is like a tree of life. (Proverbs 13:12) A soothing tongue is like a tree of life. (Proverbs 15:4) Interesting.

To do: Read Revelation 22

Repeat the memory verse several times today & repeat the first 4 weeks memory verses

Smile for the day: God is like Bounty: He is the quicker picker upper.. can handle the tough jobs.. and He won't fall apart on you.

Week 5 Day 5 <u>Memory verse:</u> "Everyone who confesses Me before men, I WILL also confess him before My Father." Matthew 10:32

<u>PROPITIATION</u>

Why do you think Jesus makes this promise? Well, let's not forget that Jesus is also our High Priest. In Hebrews 7:25-26 we are told, "therefore He is able also to save forever those who draw near to God through Him, since He always lives to make intercessions for them. For it was fitting for us to have such a high priest, holy, innocent, undefiled, separated from sinners and exalted above the heavens."

How did it come about for Jesus to be a high priest? Hebrews 2:17 says, "therefore, He had to be made like His brethren in all things, so that He might become a merciful and faithful high priest in things pertaining to God, to make propitiation for the sins of the people." It's comforting to know that "He Himself was tempted in that which He has suffered, so He is able to come to the aid of those who are tempted." (vs 18). It's comforting to me to know that He understands the temptations I've had because He was tempted also. You know it's comforting to people who have suffered various losses to be helped by others who have gone through the same thing, because they have an understanding.

To do: Read Hebrews 2
Repeat the memory verse several times today & repeat the first 4 weeks memory verses.

Smile for the day: God is like the energizer bunny. He keeps going, going and going.

KAY BRYANT

Week 5 Day 6 Review your memory verse. Record thoughts from this week's devotions and / or prayer requests.

_____

_____

_____

_____

_____

_____

_____

_____

_____

_____

_____

_____

_____

_____

_____

_____

_____

_____

_____

_____

_____

_____

_____

_____

_____

_____

_____

_____

_____

_____

_____

Week 5 Day 7 Review your memory verse. When we pray our prayers should include thanksgiving. Record here what you are thankful for today. Philippians 4:6 "Be anxious for nothing, but in everything by prayer and supplication with thanksgiving let your requests be made known to God."

_____

_____

_____

_____

_____

_____

_____

_____

_____

_____

_____

_____

_____

_____

_____

_____

_____

_____

_____

_____

_____

_____

KAY BRYANT

Week 6 Day 1 <u>Memory verse:</u> "Follow me and I WILL make you fishers of men." Matthew 4:19

<u>THE CALLING</u>

We know this promise is what Jesus said to Simon, called Peter, and his brother Andrew who were casting their fishing nets into the Sea of Galilee. Immediately they left their nets and followed Him. These were Jesus first two disciples. (Matthew 4:18-19) But, "fishers of men" is the calling all the disciples were given. In verses 21-22, Jesus calls the next two, James and John. Immediately, they left also.

What does "follow me" mean for us in this promise. Well, first of all to follow Jesus means you're not leading. It means you're keeping your eyes and attention fixed on Him. Moses was a great example of following God. In Exodus 3:10 you read about God calling Moses. Imagine - what would your reaction be if God called you to go save a nation of 600,000 people? Moses was a little intimidated at first. (verse 11) But, Jesus promises him several times that He will be leading and Moses is to follow. He also is very detailed about what Moses should say and even predicts some outcomes. In Exodus 4:12 Jesus says, "Now then go, and I, even I, will be with your mouth, and teach you what you are to say." In Exodus 4:15-16, Jesus says, "You are to speak to him (Aaron, his brother) and put the words in his mouth; and I, even I, will be with your mouth and his mouth, and I will teach you what you are to do."

To do: Read Matthew 4

Repeat the memory verse several times today & repeat the first 5 weeks memory verses

Smile for the day: God is like Dial soap. Aren't you glad you have Him? Don't you wish everybody did?

Week 6 Day 2 <u>Memory verse:</u> "Follow Me and I WILL make you fishers of men." Matthew 4:19

DISCIPLES

Moving to the New Testament, we see Jesus giving the same promise to His disciples that God gave to Moses in the Old Testament. In Mark 13:3, Peter, James, John and Andrew are questioning Jesus about what is to come. As a part of that, He says to them in verse 10, "the gospel must first be preached to all nations." This is to happen before the end time. In verse 11, He says, "when they arrest you and hand you over, do not worry beforehand about what you are to say, but say whatever is given you in that hour; for it is not you who speak, but it is the Holy Spirit." He even adds to this in Luke 21:15 by telling them that the utterance and wisdom given to them their opponents will not be able to resist or refute.

Acts 9 is about Paul's conversion. A disciple named Ananias was spoken to by the Lord in verses 11-12 where he is told to get up and go to the house of Judas and inquire about a man named Saul as he is praying and has seen in a vision that you will come, lay hands on him and he will regain his sight. Ananias had heard of Saul's reputation and was a little afraid to follow as he knew Saul had the autority to bind all Christians. But he did follow after the Lord's leading in verses 15-17.

To do: Read Acts 9

Repeat the memory verse several times today and repeat the first 5 weeks memory verses

Smile for the day: God is like Alka-Seltzer. Try Him, you'll like Him.

KAY BRYANT

Week 6 Day 3 <u>Memory verse:</u> "Follow Me and I WILL make you fishers of men. Matthew 4:19

<u>COMMITMENT</u>

How else does "follow Me" relate to us. If we are going to follow Jesus so that he can use us, we need to be totally commited to Him. Follow is defined as imitate or pursue. Think of sheep following their shepherd because he is their protector and they totally trust him and they are totally committed to him and will follow no other shepherd. Jesus says in John 10:27, "My sheep hear My voice, and I know them, and they know Me."

To me, my best Biblical role model for following is David. Plus, his word pictures paint his total transparency in talking about his feelings and emotions. "For You have been my help, and in the shadow of Your wings I sing for joy." (Psalm 63:7) David had the two pre-requisites necessary to be a true follower: he had total trust and faith in God for everything. We need to make a verbal commitment to Jesus pledging our allegiance to Him to do what He asks us to do: go and preach the gospel to all nations. A commitment is an agreement or pledge to do something showing total trust and faith.

To do: Read Psalm 63
       Repeat the memory verse several times today & repeat the first 5 weeks memory verses

Smile for the day: Coincidence is when God chooses to remain anonymous

Week 6 Day 4 <u>Memory verse:</u> **"Follow ME and I WILL make you fishers of men." Matthew 4:19**

<u>WINNER</u>

After Jesus had risen, He appeared to the 11 disciples and the last thing He said to them was,

"Go into all the world and preach the gospel to all creation." (Mark 16:15) There are only 3 things that can happen when you share your faith: (1) the person accepts Jesus as their Lord and Savior, (2) the person rejects Jesus or (3) you plant a seed. Mark Cahill in his book "One Thing You Can't Do In Heaven" says "every time we share our faith is a winning situation. Even if there is a rejection, we will be blessed for doing what we're asked to do. The only time we lose when it comes to witnessing is when we don't share our faith." Mr. Cahill also comments that 97% of church members have no involvement in any sort of evangelism. Remember from every day this week, we're promised the Holy Spirit will will guide you as to what to say and when to say it.

Romans 10:13-14 says, "Whoever will call on the name of the Lord will be saved. How then will they call on Him in whom they have not believed? And how will they believe in Him whom they have not heard? And how will they hear without a preacher?" This verse applies to all of us, not just a preacher. Part of loving your neighbor as yourself implies sharing your faith.

To do: Read Mark 16

Repeat the memory verse sevral times today & repeat the first 5 weeks memory verses

Smile for the day: The best mathematical equation I have ever seen: 1 cross + 3 nails=forgiven.

Week 6 Day 5 <u>Memory verse</u>: "Follow ME and I WILL make you fishers of men."Matthew 4:19

STEPPING OUT

The number 1 fear for being "fishers of men" is being rejected. There are others: don't know what to say, fear of losing a friend or maybe thinking you don't know enough. Two excellent resources to help you feel comfortable and know what to say are: Mark Cahill "One Thing You Can't Do In Heaven" and "Share Jesus Without Fear" by William Fay. I highly recommend both of them. They will get you motivated and excited.

Sometimes the first question is the hardest to ask. One typical one is: "may I ask you a question?" Some examples from William Fay are:

1. "Do you have any kind of spiritual belief?"
2. "To you, who is Jesus?"
3. "Do you think there is a heaven or a hell?"
4. "If you died tonight, where would you go? If heaven, ask why?"
5. "By the way, if what you are believing is not true, would you want to know?"

If yes there are tracts available that you can use for this and also to help with the follow up Jesus scriptures.

Do you remember Indiana Jones in The Last Crusade going through all kinds of deadly traps to get to the room where the potion would be to save his dad? He gets to the last trap where he is standing on the edge of a tall place looking down to a very deep chasm and where he needs to go is on the other side of the chasm with no way to get there. What does he do? He takes a step and suddenly a bridge appears for him to go across. Maybe it's time to step out in faith and take that first step. You already know by now how you will be supported.

To do: Repeat the memory verse several times today & repeat the first 5 weeks memory verses

Smile for the day: The will of God will never take you where the grace of God will not protect you

Week 6 Day 6 Review your memory verse. Record thoughts from this week's devotions and / or prayer requests.

_____

_____

_____

_____

_____

_____

_____

_____

_____

_____

_____

_____

_____

_____

_____

_____

_____

_____

_____

_____

_____

_____

_____

_____

_____

_____

Week 6 Day 7 Review your memory verse. When we pray our prayers should include thanksgiving. Record here what you are thankful for today. Philippians 4:6 "Be anxious for nothing, but in everything by prayer and supplication with thanksgiving let your requests be made known to God."

_____
_____
_____
_____
_____
_____
_____
_____
_____
_____
_____
_____
_____
_____
_____
_____
_____
_____
_____
_____
_____
_____
_____
_____
_____
_____
_____

Week 7 Day 1 <u>Memory verse:</u> "God WILL fill your mouth with laughter, and your lips with shouting." Job 8:21

<u>JOB</u>

You might be wondering why I chose this as a memory verse. I'm a firm believer in the saying "laughter is the best medicine." Over, the next few days, there will be more insights into that thought.

Now you know why I include a smile for the day every day.

In Job 8, Bildad the Shuhite is talking to Job. He speaks to Job about how God would restore the righteous estate of a man who is pure and upright. (verse 6) He implies that Job is out of sync with God. Starting in verse 11, he talks about papyrus plants that are surrounded by water, which is all they need to survive. The plant has everything it needs to survive and yet it withers. . He implies that Job is hypocritical: a man who had everything and yet is withering.

In verse 20, Bildad says God works definitely with the righteous. And, in verse 21, implies that once Job turns back to God, asks His forgiveness, God will fill Job with total joy. We will be noting a pattern this week between laughter, shouting and joy.

To do: Read Job 8

Repeat the memory verse several times today and repeat the first 6 weeks memory verses

Smile for the day: God is like a Ford. He has a better idea

Week 7 Day 2 <u>Memory verse:</u> "God WILL fill your mouth with laughter and your lips with shouting." Job 8:21

<u>PRAISE</u>

There are more references in Psalms about laughter, shouting, and joy than any other book in the Bible. Psalm 126:2 says, "then our mouth was filled with laughter and our tongue with joyful shouting." This was the reaction when the Lord brought back the captive ones of Zion. Many times through the Psalms it's mentioned that people were singing for joy as well as shouting for joy. This was always in praise for what the Lord had done.

Science has proven that laughter has benefits for the mind and body. It's essential to our well being as it has curing effects on the body, mind and emotions. Medical Science says laughter boosts your immune system and reduces blood pressure. Laughter is a stress reliever. I remember growing up we faithfully watched "I Love Lucy" every week as a family. That truly was a show that made you laugh out loud. What a great time of sharing laughter together. It's possible to say, the couple that laughs together stays together. Just a thought.

To do: Read Pslam 126

Repeat the memory verse several times today and repeat the first 6 weeks memory verses

Smile for the day: God is like General Electric. He brings good things to life

Week 7 Day 3 <u>Memory verse:</u> "God WILL fill your mouth with laughter and your lips with shouting." Job 8:21

<u>TREATMENT</u>

Chuckles and giggles are good, but they are just the beginning of laughter. There are stories of many people who give credit to laughter for healing them of various ailments. Norman Cousins was diagnosed to be terminally ill. He had a 1 in 500 chance of surviving. He decided to do what I call the "Laughter Treatment." Daily he watched funny movies, funny tv shows, and read funny books. He wrote a book about this titled "Anatomy Of An Illness." Mr. Cousins survived. You can ask friends to call you with a good joke. Jokes are a great way to lighten up your day. I read that children laugh 300 times a day while adults laugh less than 15 times a day. I'm sure Norman was close to laughing 300 times a day.

Psalm 98:6b says, "shout joyfully before the King, the Lord." Pastor Joel Osteen says "when you have a joyful spirit constantly on the inside, health and healing are flowering." He goes on to give a challenge for every day: "at least 3 times a day find something that makes you laugh out loud."

To do: Read Psalm 98

Repeat the memory verse several times today & repeat the first 6 weeks memory verses

Smile for the day: God is like the U.S. Post Office. Neither rain, nor snow, nor sleet nor ice will keep Him from His appointed destination.

Week 7 Day 4 <u>Memory verse:</u> "God **WILL** fill your mouth with laughter and your lips with shouting." Job 8:21

<u>SHOUT</u>

Bible verses about shouting were always a form of praise to the Lord for something. Here are some examples: "Shout joyfully to God, all the earth. Sing the glory of His name; make His praise glorious." (Psalm 66:1,2) Psalm 95:1-3 says, " O come let us sing for joy to the Lord, let us shout joyfully to the rock of our salvation. Let us come before His presence with Thanksgiving, let us shout joyfully to Him with psalms."

Shouting was a physical response of joy. Rejoicing is an inner response of joy. Psalm 35:9 says, "And my soul shall rejoice in the Lord; it shall exult in His salvation." Philippians 3:1 says, "Finally, my brethren, rejoice in the Lord" And, Philippians 4:4 says, "rejoice in the Lord always, again, I will say rejoice." Matthew 2:10 describes the shepherds reaction when they saw the star that guided them to Bethlehem, "when they saw the star, they rejoiced exceedingly with great joy."

Laughter, shouting and rejoicing should be a part of our lives as we walk with the Lord. We should rejoice with Thanksgiving. In doing so our hearts and souls and minds are dwelling on all of God's blessings throughout our lives.

To do: Read Philippians 4
Repeat the memory verse several times today & repeat the first 6 weeks of memory verses

Smile for the day: How do they figure out the price of hammers? Per pound

Week 7 Day 5 <u>Memory verse:</u> "God WILL fill your mouth with laughter and your lips with shouting." Job 8:21

<u>JOY</u>

Laughter and shouting come from a joyful spirit. Here are some verses regarding a joyful heart and a joyful spirit. Matthew describes Jesus entry into Jerusalem in Matthew 21:9, "the crowds were shouting Hosanna to the Son of David. Blessed is He who comes in the name of the Lord." You can sense their joy as he entered on a donkey. Most of them spread their coats in the road and cut branches from the trees to spread on the road. Try to visualize this. Pretend you were there.

There are 214 uses of the word joy in the Bible. Joy is a gift from God and it is a fruit of the spirit. (Galations 5:22) Proverbs 15:13 says, "a joyful heart makes a cheerful face" And, Proverbs 17:22 says, "a joyful heart is good medicine." Even God shouts with joy. Zephaniah 3:17 says, "The Lord your God is in your midst... He will exult over you with joy, He will be quiet in His love, He will rejoice over you with shouts of joy." Dwight L. Moody says: "Joy is not a season, it's a way of living. Joy is not necessarily the absence of suffering, it is the presence of God."

Try to remember a time when you shouted for joy. I remember throwing my cap in the air and shouting for joy at the end of my college graduation ceremony. I remember standing up and shouting for joy when both our son and our daughter made their first soccer goal. My absolute favorite praise song is "Shout To The Lord" written and performed by Darlene Zscheck. Trust me I want to stand up and dance to this song. It truly fills me with joy.

To do: Read Matthew 21:1-16

Repeat the memory verse several times today & repeat the first 6 weeks memory verses

Smile for the day: God is like Chevrolet. The heartbeat of America

SHOUT TO THE LORD
by Darlene Zscheck

My Jesus, My Savior
Lord there is none like You
All of my days I want to praise
the wonders of Your mighty love

My comfort, my shelter
Tower of refuge and strength
Let every breath, all that I am
Never cease to worship You

Refrain:

Shout to the Lord all the earth, let us sing
Power and majesty, praise to the King
Mountains bow down and the seas will roar
At the sound of Your name

I sing for joy at the work of Your hands
Forever I'll love You, forever I'll stand
Nothing compares to the promise I have in You

Week 7 Day 6 Review your memory verse. Record thoughts from this week's devotions and / or prayer requests.

_____
_____
_____
_____
_____
_____
_____
_____
_____
_____
_____
_____
_____
_____
_____
_____
_____
_____
_____
_____
_____
_____
_____

KAY BRYANT

Week 7 Day 7 Review your memory verse. When we pray our prayers should include thanksgiving. Record here what you are thankful for today. Philippians 4:6 "Be anxious for nothing, but in everything by prayer and supplication with thanksgiving let your requests be made known to God."

_____
_____
_____
_____
_____
_____
_____
_____
_____
_____
_____
_____
_____
_____
_____
_____
_____
_____
_____
_____
_____
_____
_____
_____
_____

Week 8 Day 1 <u>Memory verse:</u> "He WILL wipe away every tear from their eyes; and there will be no longer death, mourning, crying or pain." Revelation 21:4

<u>THE VISION</u>

Revelation 21 is about the New Jerusalem and the disciple John is sharing the vision of it that the Lord gave him. As you read Revelation 21 you're going to wish that somehow you could have a picture in color of the glorious city described. Note in verses 6 and 7 several more promises. "I will give to the one who thirsts from the spring of the water of life without cost. He who overcomes will inherit these things and I will be His Lord and he will be My son." Isaiah 49:13b says, "For the Lord has comforted His people and will have compassion on His afflicted." More reinforcement in Psalm 9:9, " The Lord also will be a stronghold for the oppressed, a stronghold in times of trouble."

Reading Revelation 21 is mind boggling because it's beyond our imagination. I love the picture portrayed in verse 23: "and the city has no need of the sun or the moon to shine on it, for the glory of God has illumined it, and its lamp is the Lamb."

To do: Read Revelation 21

Repeat the memory verse several times today & repeat the first 7 weeks memory verses

Smile for the day: Blessed are the flexible for they shall not be bent out of shape

Week 8 Day 2 <u>Memory verse:</u> "He WILL wipe away every tear from their eyes; and there will be no longer death, mourning, crying or pain." Revelation 21:4

<u>TEARS</u>

What a blessed promise to wipe away every tear. Isaiah 30 reinforces this promise even more.

Verses 18 and 19 say: "therefore the Lord longs to be gracious to you and therefore He waits on high to have compassion on you. For the Lord is a God of justice; how blessed are all those who long for Him. O people in Zion, inhabitant in Jerusalem, you will weep no longer. He will surely be gracious to you at the sound of your cry. He hears it, He will answer you." And he will respond as in Psalm 147:3, "He heals the brokenhearted and binds up their wounds."

Most adults can remember as children their mothers and fathers wiping away tears from their eyes, usually embracing them and thus comforting them. So this promise offers comfort and a feeling of being embraced by God's love. When we have hope, this is one of the hopes we have to look forward to. It assures us that God is aware of every tear we have ever shed in discomfort and He is the solution for all those tears.

To do: Read Psalm 147

Repeat the memory verse several times today & repeat the first 7 weeks memory verses

Smile for the day: God wants spiritual fruit, not religious nuts

Week 8 Day 3 <u>Memory verse:</u> "He WILL wipe away every tear from your eyes; and there will no longer be death, mourning, crying or pain." Revelation 21:4

PROPHECY

In Luke 4:17-19, Jesus was at the synagogue in Nazareth and the book of Isaiah was handed to Him. He opened the book and found the place where it was written: "The Spirit of the Lord was upon Me, because He anointed Me to preach the gospel to the poor. He has sent Me to proclaim the release to the captives, and recovery to the blind, to set free those who are oppressed, to proclaim the favorable year of the Lord." In verse 21 He says, "today this scripture has been fulfilled in your hearing."

So Isaiah 61:1-2 is the prophecy made in the Old Testament, fulfilled by Jesus in the New Testament. Isaish 61:3 goes on to illuminate this prophecy even more and shows what you get instead: "to grant those who mourn in Zion (referring to His second coming), giving them a garland instead of ashes (picture a crown or a wreath of flowers as opposed to ashes – sins you've committed), the oil of gladness instead of mourning, (referring to a perfumed ointment poured on guests at joyous feasts (Psalm 23:5), the mantle of praise instead of a spirit of fainting, (garments of praise were bright colored garments indicating thankfulness)." This is definitely something to look forward to.

To do: Read Isaiah 61

Repeat the memory verse several times today & repeat the first 7 weeks memory verses

Smile for the day: There is no key to happiness. The door is always open

KAY BRYANT

Week 8 Day 4 <u>Memory verse:</u> "He will wipe away every tear from your eyes; and there will no longer be death, mourning, crying or pain." Revelation 21:4

DEATH

Here are some verses to reinforce this promise for you. Isaiah 60:20 says, "Your sun will no longer set, nor will your moon wane, for you will have the Lord for an everlasting light, and the days of your mourning will be over." I Corinthians 15:26 says, " the last enemy that will be abolished is death." II Timothy 1:10 refers to the "appearing of our Savior Christ Jesus, who abolished death and brought life and immortality to light through the gospel." God speaks in Isaiah 65:19 about creating a new Jerusalem that He will rejoice in. "There will no longer be heard in her the voice of weeping and the sound of crying."

I hope you find comfort and encouragement in these verses and that just reading them gives you a sense of peace. There will no longer be death, mourning, crying or pain because there will no longer be any sins or evil present. Wow. That in itself is something to look forward to. You will find Ist Corinthians chapter 15 to be highly enlightening as Paul is speaking, preaching the gospel. When I read scriptures about Paul speaking, I imagine him to be a very charismatic speaker. He says in verses 54 and 55, "Death is swallowed up in victory. O death, where is your victory? O death, where is your sting?"

To do: Read I Corinthians 15

Repeat the memory verse several times today & repeat the first 7 weeks memory verses

Smile for the day: Do the math …. count your blessings.

Week 8 Day 5 <u>Memory verse:</u> "He WILL wipe away every tear from your eyes, and there will no longer be death, mourning, crying or pain." Revelation 21:4

ANTICIPATION

Let's end up this week with a lovely picture of when this promise is fulfilled. Two verses that are almost identical. Isaiah 51:11: "So the ransomed of the Lord will return and come with joyful shouting to Zion, and everlasting joy will be on their heads. They will attain gladness and joy and sorrow and sighing will flee away." And, Isaiah 35:10: "And the ransomed of the Lord will return and come with joyful shouting to Zion, with everlasting joy upon their heads. They will find gladness and joy, and sorrow and sighing will fade away."

Isaiah 35 is a great chapter to end this week on. It is a lovely picturesque of what will happen when God comes, like: "the eyes of the blind will be opened, and the ears of the deaf will be unstopped, the lame will leap like a deer and the tongue of the mute will shout for joy." (verses 5,6) Praise the Lord. And by now, I'm sure you are picking up on every verse that has the word "will" in it, which is obviously indicative of more promises.

To do: Read Isaish 35

Repeat the memory verse several times today and repeat the first 7 weeks memory verses

Smile for the day: Dear God, I have a problem, it's me.

Week 8 Day 6 Review your memory verse. Record thoughts from this week's devotions and / or prayer requests.

_____
_____
_____
_____
_____
_____
_____
_____
_____
_____
_____
_____
_____
_____
_____
_____
_____
_____
_____
_____
_____
_____
_____
_____
_____
_____
_____
_____
_____
_____

Week 8 Day 7 Review your memory verse. When we pray our prayers should include thanksgiving. Record here what you are thankful for today. Philippians 4:6 "Be anxious for nothing, but in everything by prayer and supplication with thanksgiving let your requests be made known to God."

_____

_____

_____

_____

_____

_____

_____

_____

_____

_____

_____

_____

_____

_____

_____

_____

_____

_____

_____

_____

_____

_____

_____

_____

Week 9 Day 1 <u>Memory verse:</u> "If you keep My commandments, you WILL abide in My love." John 15:10

<u>KEEP</u>

First, let's clarify what "keep" means. Keep means to fulfill, to guard, to observe, to take care of, to continue doing something. So to keep Jesus's commandments, we are to possess them permanently. This promise verse is reinforced in John 14:15: "If you love Me, you will keep My commandments." In John 15:10b, Jesus adds to today's memory verse by saying, "just as I have kept My Father's commandments and abide in His love."

And what is the definition of commandment. A commandment is like an instruction or an order given. I John 2:3 reiterates our memory verse: "By this we know that we have come to know Him, if we keep His commandments." In Matthew 19:16 someone comes to Jesus and says, "Teacher, what good thing shall I do that I may obtain eternal life?" Jesus responds, "Why are you asking Me about what is good? There is only one who is good; but if you wish to enter into life, keep the commandments."(vs 17)

To do: Read John 15

Repeat the memory verse several times today & repeat the first 8 weeks memory verses

Smile for the day: Faith is the ability to not panic

GREATEST

A lawyer asked Jesus in Matthew 22:36, "Which is the great commandment in the law?

And He said to him, "You shall love the Lord your God with all your heart, and with all your soul and with all your mind." (verse 37) Did you see the word shall following you? That's a promise you make to the Lord. In Exodus 20 Moses is reading the 10 commandments given to him by God to the people for the first time. The 1st commandment of the law says, "You shall have no other gods before me" (verse 3) which means you shall love the Lord your God with all your heart, soul and mind. By the way, I've often thought how sin was never identified until the commandments were given. At that point in time there was a reference as to what sin was and wasn't. Who are what do you love with all your heart, soul and mind? If it's Jesus, you will never be disappointed.

To do: Exodus 20

Repeat the memory verse several times today and repeat the first 8 weeks memory verses

Smile for the day: If you worry, you didn't pray. If you prayed, don't worry.

KAY BRYANT

Week 9 Day 3 <u>Memory verse:</u> "If you keep My commandments, you WILL abide in My love." John 15:10

<u>ABIDE</u>

In John 15, Jesus follows up His statements about the vine and the branches in verse 4: "Abide in Me and I in you as the branch cannot bear fruit of itself unless it abides in the vine, so neither can you unless you abide in Me." In I John 3:22, we read, "and whatever we ask we receive from Him, because we keep His commandments and do the things that are pleasing in His sight." This promise tells us if we do His will, He hears us. Be careful here in your interpretation. The clue is if you're abiding in Him, meaning he's directing you, your thoughts, your motives and your desires. This verse is not to be taken literally wishing for things like more money, a bigger house, a better job, etc.

In I John 2:6, the disciple John writes, "the one who says he abides in Him ought himself to walk in the same manner as He walked." I John 3:24 says, "The one who keeps His commandments abides in Him, and He in him. We know that He abides in us, by the Spirit whom He has given us."

To do: Read I John 2

Repeat the memory verse several times today & repeat the first 8 weeks memory verses

Smile for the day: The Son is shining and He can certainly use you

Week 9 Day 4 <u>Memory verse</u>: "If you keep My commandments, you WILL abide in My love." John 15:10

<u>SECOND</u>

After giving the greatest commandment, Jesus says "the second is like the first, you shall love your neighbor as yourself. On these two commandments depend the whole law and the Prophets." (Matthew 22:39-40) (Galations 5:14) This is reinforced in Matthew 7:12, "in everything, therefore, treat people the same way you want them to treat you, for this is the law and the prophets." How do we love one another? One way is mentioned in Galations 6:2, "bear one another's burdens and thereby fulfill the law of Christ." Romans 15:1-2 say,s "Now we who are strong ought to bear the weaknesses of those without strength and not just please ourselves." Each of us to to please his neighbor for his good, to his edification." Notice again the word shall in Matthew 22:39. It follows the word you.

Romans 13:8 says, "Owe nothing to anyone except to love one another; for he who loves his neighbor has fulfilled the law." The Law refers to what was given to Moses in the Old Testament. "Whatever was written in earlier times was writen for our instruction, so that through perseverance and the encouragement of the scriptures, we might have hope." (Romans 15: 4) Hebrews 8:6 speaks of the New Covenant: "But, now He (Jesus) has obtained a more excellent ministry, by as much as He is also the mediator of a better covenant,which has been enacted on better promises."

To do: Read Hebrews 8

Repeat the memory verse several times today & repeat the first 8 weeks memory verses

Smile for the day: As a child of God, prayer is kind of like calling home everyday

Week 9 Day 5 <u>Memory verse</u>: "If you keep My commandments, you WILL abide in My love." John 15:10

<u>GOAL</u>

To abide in Jesus love – that is the goal. In John 14:21, Jesus says, "He who has my commandments and keeps them is the one who loves Me; and he who loves Me will be loved by My Father, and I will love him and will disclose Myself to him."

What is the love that we will abide in? I Corinthians is the love chapter of the New Testament; these are the things it says love is:

1. Love is patient

2. Love is kind
3. Love does not brag
4. Love is not arrogant
5. Love does not act unbecomingly
6. Love does not seek its own
7. Love is not provoked
8. Love does not take into account a wrong suffered

9. Love does not rejoice in unrighteousness
10. Love rejoices with the truth
11. Love bears all things
12. Love believes all things
13. Love hopes all things
14. Love endures all things
15. Love never fails

To do: Read I Corinthians 13
    Repeat the memory verse several times today & repeat the first 8 weeks memory verses

Smile for the day: In the circle of God's love, He's waiting to use your full potential

Week 9 Day 6 Review your memory verse. Record thoughts from this week's devotions and / or prayer requests.

_____

_____

_____

_____

_____

_____

_____

_____

_____

_____

_____

_____

_____

_____

_____

_____

_____

_____

_____

_____

_____

_____

_____

_____

KAY BRYANT

Week 9 Day 7 Review your memory verse. When we pray our prayers should include thanksgiving. Record here what you are thankful for today. Philippians 4:6 "Be anxious for nothing, but in everything by prayer and supplication with thanksgiving let your requests be made known to God."

_____

_____

_____

_____

_____

_____

_____

_____

_____

_____

_____

_____

_____

_____

_____

_____

_____

_____

_____

_____

_____

_____

Week 10 Day 1 <u>Memory verse:</u> "Jesus said, do not judge so that you WILL not be judged." Matthew 7:1

<u>MEASURE</u>

Jesus goes on to say in verse 2 that the way you judge is how you will be judged. Whatever your standard of measure, that's how you will be measured. Judging others takes into account only one perspective – ours. We focus on some quality, behavior, dress, words, lifestyle, etc. of another person that we choose to let irritate us to the point that we don't see the flaw in ourselves. Jesus describes this in verse 4 as, "How can you say to your brother, 'let me take the speck out of your eye, and behold the log is in your own eye?'" This makes us a hypocrite. Unfortunately, this is one of the major criticisms non-Christians have about Christians.

Remember, last week we talked about loving our neighbor as ourselves. Part of the way we do that is to treat people the way we want to be treated. (Matthew 7:12) So, reverse roles for a minute. Pretend you are the other person and that person is you. One of the first things to do when you realize you are being judgmental is to pray about it. Ask the Lord to give you a non-judgmental spirit. Try looking for a positive or two in the other person. Trust me, you should be able to find at least one. There are a lot of people who don't realize they are being judgmental. They have an immediate first reaction and live with it, without questioning it, like instant responses when seeing a homeless person or an obese person. We need to take a frequent inventory of any judgmental responses to others.

To do: Read Matthew 7

Repeat the memory verse several times today & repeat the first 9 weeks memory verses

Smile for the day: Growing old is inevitable. . . growing up is optional.

Week 10 Day 2 <u>Memory verse</u>: "Jesus said, do not judge so that you WILL not be judged." Matthew 7:1

PERSPECTIVE

When King David and his servants were on their way to Bahurim as they were fleeing Absalom, a man named Shimei of the family of Saul came out cursing them and throwing stones. It was so offensive and so continuous that David's servants wanted to go cut off his head. (II Samuel 16:5-8) David responded to let him alone and let him curse. (verse 11) The non-judgmental behavior on King David's part continued in II Samuel 19:16-19 when Shimei comes with 1000 Benjamites to meet David. Shimei falls down before the King and asks for his forgiveness and confesses his sin before David. Again David is advised to put this man to death because "he cursed the Lord's anointed."(verse 21) But David is returning to Jerusalem in glory as the King, after Absalom was defeated. And David says, "should any man be put to death in Israel today?" (verse 22) It was a day of celebration. David chose to focus on what was important in the overall picture rather than being judgmental about an affront. David chose the right perspective. Sometimes that's all we need - change our perspective.

To do: Read II Samuel 19
Repeat the memory verse several times today & repeat the first 9 weeks memory verses

Smile for the day: Silence is often misinterpreted, but never misquoted

Week 10 Day 3 <u>Memory verse:</u> "Jesus said, do not judge so that you WILL not be judged." Matthew 7

<u>OBSTACLE</u>

Romans 14:13 says, "Let us not judge one another anymore, but rather determine this – not to put an obstacle or a stumbling block in a brother's way." What this points out to me is in our church family we have both new and seasoned Christians and misunderstandings and disagreements are bound to happen. We don't want to be a stumbling block for a new believing brother. We need to be suppportive.

All of Romans 14 is about not judging others. Many of the verses have to do with eating habits, comparing what one person does to what another does. Verse 17-18 says, "the kingdom of God is not eating and drinking, but righteousness and peace and joy in the Holy Spirit. For he who in this way serves Christ is acceptable to God and approved by men." Focus on the right things. We are to "pursue the things which make for peace and the building up one another." (verse 19)

To do: Read Romans 14

Repeat the memory verse several times today & repeat the first 9 weeks memory verses

Smile for the day: A Sunday school teacher was discussing the 10 Commandments with her six year olds. After explaining the commandment to honor thy father and mother, she asked "is there a commandment that teaches us how to treat our brothers and sisters?" Without missing a beat, one little boy answered, "thou shall not kill."

Week 10 Day 4 <u>Memory verse:</u> "Jesus said, do not judge so that you
WILL not be judged." Matthew 7

MERCIFUL

Luke 6:36 says, "be merciful, just as your Father is merciful."
Mercy is showing compassion to an offender who doesn't deserve kindness. This verse is immediately followed by Luke 6:37 which says, "do
not judge and you will not be judged; and do not condemn, and you
will not be condemned; pardon and you will be pardoned." Also, don't
make hasty decisions. I remember when our daughter was in 2nd grade
and her teacher sent a note home about an unfortunate class incident
and accused our daughter of being the problem. I believed the teacher
and chastized our daughter, only to find out later that our daughter
was innocent. Luke 6:28 says, "bless those who curse you, pray for
those who mistreat you." Wow. That's a doozy of a request, isn't it? All
of us have at least one graphic memory of someone who cursed us or
mistreated us and praying for that person was not even close to being
our first response.

To do: Read Luke 6
Repeat the memory verse several times today & repeat the first
9 weeks memory verses

Smile for the day: A Sunday school teacher asked, "do you think Noah
did a lot of fishing when he was on the ark? "No, replied Johnny. How
could he with just 2 worms?"

Week 10 Day 5 <u>Memory verse:</u> "Jesus said, do not judge so that you WILL not be judged." Matthew 7:1

<u>REVIEW</u>

Let's review what we've learned this week about judging others.
1. To judge is to form an estimate, a conclusion or evaluation about something or somone
2. How we judge others is how we'll be judged
3. To not judge, we need to treat others the way we want to be treated
4. To not judge, we need to change our perspective
5. To not judge, we need to not be a stumbling block, but a supporter
6. To not judge, we need to be merciful, to pray for those who hurt us

All of these things reinforce the Second Commandment: "Love your neighbor as yourself." Also, all of the above are very humbling. A humble person is a modest person. Dr. David Jeremiah has said, "being humble doesn't mean you think less of yourself. It means you think of yourself less."

Luke 14:11 says, "For everyone who exalts himself will be humbled, and he who humbles himself will be exalted.'

To do: Read Luke 14
        Repeat the memory verse several times today & repeat the first 9 weeks memory verses

Smile for the day: A Sunday School teacher asked her class why Joseph and Mary took Jesus with them to Jerusalem. A small child replied, "they couldn't get a baby-sitter."

Week 10 Day 6 Review your memory verse. Record thoughts from this week's devotions and / or prayer requests.

_____

_____

_____

_____

_____

_____

_____

_____

_____

_____

_____

_____

_____

_____

_____

_____

_____

_____

_____

_____

_____

_____

_____

_____

_____

_____

_____

Week 10 Day 7 Review your memory verse. When we pray our prayers should include thanksgiving. Record here what you are thankful for today. Philippians 4:6 "Be anxious for nothing, but in everything by prayer and supplication with thanksgiving let your requests be made known to God."

_____

_____

_____

_____

_____

_____

_____

_____

_____

_____

_____

_____

_____

_____

_____

_____

_____

_____

_____

_____

_____

_____

KAY BRYANT

Week 11 Day 1 <u>Memory verse:</u> **"Know that I WILL pour out my Spirit on you. I WILL make My words known to you." Proverbs 1:23**

MEDITATE

One way God makes his words known to us is through His word. But for His words to be known to us requires that we meditate on His word, not just read it. Biblically meditate means to be thinking, asking how to apply, what's best for me, show any sins to be confessed. The first part of vs 23 says, "turn to My reproof." That's a pre-requisite for this week's promise above. In Proverbs 1:2-3 Solomon defines his purpose for writing Proverbs: (1) "<u>to know</u> wisdom and instruction;" (2) "<u>to discern</u> the sayings of understanding;" (3) "<u>to receive</u> instruction in wise behavior, righteousness, justice and equity." Proverbs 15:5 says, "he who regards reproof is sensible."

Meditation on scripture is where you can feel God's presence as you ask Him for His guidance in reading scripture and how to apply what you read to how you live. Be sure you are in a quiet place where you won't be interrupted. I pray before I read the Bible that God will show me what He has for me for today. Then, instead of just reading scripture like a book, I have a purpose. I'm looking for a gem of wisdom to apply to my day and my life. This changes my outlook on daily being in the word.

To do: Read Proverbs 1

Repeat the memory verse several times today & repeat the first 10 weeks memory verses

Smile for the day: A child asked his mother why the bride was wearing white. She said, 'because white is the color of happiness.' He then asked why the groom was wearing black.

Week 11 Day 2 <u>Memory verse:</u> **"Know that I WILL pour out my Spirit on you. I WILL make My words known to you." Proverbs 1:23**

PENTECOST

How and when did the disciples receive the Holy Spirit? Jesus appeared to the 11 disciples (later known as apostles) the first time the day after His resurrection. They rejoiced when they saw the Lord and He showed them both His hands and His side. (John 20:20) In John: 20:21, Jesus says, "as the Father has sent Me, I also send you." Luke tells us in Acts 1:2, that "He was taken up to heaven, after He had by the Holy Spirit given orders to the apostles whom He had chosen." They did not actually receive the Holy Spirit at this time. In acts 1:4 Jesus instructed the apostles not to leave Jerusalem but to wait "for John baptized with water, but you will be baptized with the Holy Spirit not many days from now." (verse 5)

The Day of Pentecost is the day all believers at that time received the Holy Spirit. (Acts 2:1-4) They had to wait til Christ was glorified before receiving the Holy Spirit. Pentecost is a Jewish feast held 50 days after Passover, celebrating the beginning of the wheat harvest in May or early June. In the Old Testament it is referred to as the Feast of the Harvest, one of 3 major feasts held per year. It was a major celebration that everyone turned out for. There was no work on this day.

To do: Read Acts 1

Repeat the memory verse several times today & repeat the first 10 weeks memory verses

Smile for the day: So your mother says prayers for you each night. What does she say? "Thank God he's in bed.

KAY BRYANT

Week 11 Day 3 <u>Memory verse:</u> "Know that I WILL pour out my Spirit on you. I WILL make My words known to you." Proverbs 1:23

<u>POUR OUT</u>

Pour out My Spirit upon Him was a prophecy from God given to Isaiah the prophet referring to Jesus. (Isaiah 42:1) Matthew 12:18 refers to this prophecy: "Behold My Servant whom I have chosen; My Beloved in whom My Soul is well pleased; I will put my Spirit upon Him and He shall proclaim justice to the gentiles." Jesus was baptized by His cousin, John the Baptist. Matthew 3:16 says, "After being baptized, the heavens were opened, and he (John) saw the Spirit of God descending as a dove and lighting on Him." Jesus was baptized because it was fitting to fulfill all righteousness. (Matthew 3:15) Jesus' baptism symbolized His coming death and resurrection. Baptism would become the pattern that future saints were to follow as a symbol of their faith.

And, we receive the same. In Acts 2:38, Peter says, "repent, and each of you be baptized in the name of Jesus Christ for the forgiveness of your sins and you will receive the gift of the Holy Spirit."

Wow! And look at this assurance: John 14:16, "I will ask the Father and He will give you another Helper, that He may be with you forever." What a promise.

To do: Read Acts 2

Repeat the memory verse several times today & repeat the first 10 weeks memory verses

Smile for the day: Do not worry about old age. It doesn't last.

Week 11 Day 4 <u>Memory verse:</u> "Know that I WILL pour out my Spirit on you. I WILL make My words known to you." Proverbs 1:23

<u>SCRIPTURES</u>

God will make His words known to us through the scriptures, which started in the Old Testament. In II Chronicles 34, during the reign of King Josiah, when the workmen were rebuilding the house of God, Hilkiah the priest found the Book of the Law of the Lord given by Moses. (verse 14) When it was read to King Josiah, he tore his clothes. (verse 19) He then read the book to all the inhabitants of Jerusalem and all of Jerusalem did according to the covenant of God. (verse 32)

Psalm 19:7-9 says, "The <u>law of the Lord</u> is perfect, restoring the soul; the <u>testimony of the Lord</u> is sure, making wise the simple; the <u>precepts of the Lord</u> are right, rejoicing the heart; the <u>commandment of the Lord</u> is pure, enlightening the eyes; the <u>fear of the Lord i</u>s clean, enduring forever; the <u>judgments of the Lord</u> are true, they are righteous altogether." These are the some of the words God makes known to us in scripture and their benefits.

To do: Read Psalm 19

Repeat the memory verse several times today and repeat the first 10 weeks memory verses

Smile for the day: I got a job at a bakery because I kneaded the dough

Week 11 Day 5 <u>Memory verse:</u> "**Know that I WILL pour out my Spirit on you. I WILL make My words known to you.**" **Proverbs 1:23**

<u>INSPIRED</u>

While we know that God makes His words known to us through Scripture, we need to also know that the Bible is the inspired Word of God and is timeless. II Peter 1:20-21 says, "But know this first of all, that no prophecy of Scripture is a matter of one's own interpretation, for no prophecy was ever made by an act of the human will, but men moved by the Holy Spirit spoke from God." And, II Timothy 3:16-17 says, "All scripture is inspired by God and profitable for teaching, for reproof, for corrections, for training in righteousness so that the man of God may be equipped for every good work." Isaiah 40:8 says, "the grass withers, the flower fades, but the Word of God stands forever."

Romans 15:4 says, " For whatever was written in earlier times was written for our instruction, so that through perseverance and the encouragement of the scriptures we might have hope." One suggestion, if you are doing a journal during your devotional time, is to write down each day one encouraging or inspiring verse for you for that day. Think about that verse throughout the day.

To do: Read II Timothy 3
Repeat the memory verse several times today & repeat the first 10 weeks memory verses

Smile for the day: Why were the Indians here first? They had reservations.

Would like to add the following passage of scripture from Psalms 119:97-105, where David is speaking about the word of God:

"Oh how I love your law!
It is my meditation all the day.
Your commandments make me wiser
than my enemies, For they are mine.
I have more insight than all my teachers,
For Your testimonies are my meditation.
I understand more than the aged,
Because I have observed Your precepts.
I have restrained my feet from every evil way,
That I may keep Your word.
I have not turned aside from Your ordinances,
For You Yourself have taught me.
How sweet are Your words to my taste!
Yes, sweeter than honey to my mouth!
From Your precepts I get understanding;
Therefore I hate every false way."

"Your word is a lamp to my feet and a light to my path."

Week 11 Day 6 Review your memory verse. Record thoughts from this week's devotions and / or prayer requests.

_____

_____

_____

_____

_____

_____

_____

_____

_____

_____

_____

_____

_____

_____

_____

_____

_____

_____

_____

_____

_____

_____

_____

_____

_____

_____

_____

_____

Week 11 Day 7 Review your memory verse. When we pray our prayers should include thanksgiving. Record here what you are thankful for today. Philippians 4:6 "Be anxious for nothing, but in everything by prayer and supplication with thanksgiving let your requests be made known to God."

_____

_____

_____

_____

_____

_____

_____

_____

_____

_____

_____

_____

_____

_____

_____

_____

_____

_____

_____

_____

_____

_____

_____

_____

Week 12 Day 1 <u>Memory verse:</u> "Let us not lose heart in doing good, for in due time we WILL reap if we don't grow weary." Galations 6:9

<u>FOCUS</u>

Paul is encouraging believers in Galations 6 to bear one another's burdens, as well as our own load as each of us will reap what we sow. He encourages us to "do good to all people " (vs 10) and to not give up. How can we do good and not give up? (1) First, we "fix our eyes on Jesus, the author and perfector of our faith, who for the joy set before Him endured the cross." (Hebrews 12:2) "For consider Him who has endured such hostility by sinners Himself, so that you will not grow weary and lose heart." (Hebrews 12:3)

(2) We need a goal, something we're striving towards: to become more and more like Jesus.

(3) We need commitment to that goal, something that compels us to keep moving. The Word of God and memorizing scripture encourage us to keep moving.

(4) We need prayer as it connects us to our source of strength to keep us on track with our goals, commitments and time in the Word. Pray for God's guidance and timing.

To do: Read Galations 6

Repeat the memory verse several times today and repeat the first 11 weeks memory verses

Smile for the day: I'm reading a book about anti-gravity. I just can't put it down

Week 12 Day 2 <u>Memory verse:</u> "Let us not lose heart in doing good, for in due time we WILL reap if we don't grow weary." Galations 6:9

DON'T GIVE UP

If you are a major sports fan of football, baseball, basketball, soccer, etc., I'm sure you've watched games where your team was losing so badly to the other team that you lost heart. Fortunately, most athletes in these sports play their hearts out and don't lose heart or give up. And, there have been miracle games where the team behind ends up winning. So, this is how we are to live the Christian life. We are to run the race and not give up. Hebrews 12:1 says, "Therefore, since we have so great a cloud of witnesses surrounding us, let us also lay aside every encumbrance and the sin which so easily entangles us, and let us run with endurance the race that is set before us."

In II Corinthians 4:16, Paul says, "Therefore, we do not lose heart, but though our outer man is decaying, yet our inner man is being renewed day by day." How is it being renewed? Colossians 3:10-11 says, "put on the new self who is being renewed to a true knowledge according to the image of the One who created him – Christ is all in all."

To do: Read Hebrews 12

Repeat the memory verse several times today and repeat the first 11 weeks memory verses

Smile for the day: Broken pencils are pointless

Week 12 Day 3 <u>Memory verse:</u> **"Let us not lose heart in doing good, for in due time we WILL reap if we don't grow weary." Galations 6:9**

<u>ENDURANCE</u>

There is another thing you need to not lose heart in doing good and this is endurance. Endurance is tied to what we will reap. Hebrews 10:36 says, "For you have need of endurance, so that when you have done the will of God, you may receive what was promised." James says in James 5:11, "You have heard of the endurance of Job and have seen the outcome of the Lord's dealings, that the Lord is full of compassion and is merciful." You will note in Job 2:10, Job is speaking to his wife who is encouraging him to curse God and die and Job says, "shall we indeed accept good from God and not accept adversity." Adversity is another hiccup that can cause us to lose heart.

We can take encouragement from I Corinthians 15:58, "Therefore my beloved brethren, be steadfast, immovable, always abounding in the work of the Lord, knowing that your toil is not in vain in the Lord."

To do: Read James 5
Repeat the memory verse several times today and repeat the first 11 weeks memory verses

Smile for the day: They told me I had type-A blood, but it was a type-O

Week 12 Day 4 <u>Memory verse:</u> "Let us not lose heart in doing good, for in due time we WILL reap if we don't grow weary." Galations 6:9

<u>LIGHT</u>

The apostle Paul is the perfect example of someone who just didn't grow weary. He speaks in II Corinthians 4 about doing good, about sharing the gospel. In verse 6, he says, "For God, who said, 'light shall shine out of darkness,' is the One who has shone in our hearts to give the Light of the knowledge of the glory of God in the face of Christ." He goes on to say in verses 8 and 9, "we are afflicted in every way, but not crushed; perplexed, but not despairing; persecuted, but not forsaken; struck down, but not destroyed." In verse 17 Paul gives this assurance, " for momentary, light affliction is producing for us an eternal weight of glory far beyond all comparison."

Paul, in speaking to the Christians in Colasse, says in Colossians 1:10, "walk in a manner worthy of the Lord, to please Him in all respects, bearing fruit in every good work and increasing in the knowledge of God." Matthew says in Matthew 5:16, "Let your light shine before men in such a way that they may see your good works, and glorify your Father who is in heaven." We are to shine like stars in the universe. Daniel says in Daniel 12:3, "those who have insight will shine brightly like the brightness of the expanse of heaven, and those who lead the many to righteousness like the stars forever and ever."

To do: Read II Corinthians 4
Repeat the memory verse several times today & repeat the first 11 weeks memory verses

Smile for the day: A cartoonist was found dead in his home. Details are sketchy

Week 12 Day 5 <u>Memory verse:</u> "Let us not lose heart in doing good, for the due time we WILL reap if we don't grow weary." Galations 6:9

<u>REAP</u>

In II Timothy 4, Paul is writing to Timothy giving him words of encouragement and guidance. In verse 5 he says, "endure hardship, do the work of an evangelist, fulfill your ministry." One of my favorite verses in the Bible is verse 7, "I have fought the good fight, I have finished the course, I have kept the faith." Wow. That's a goal worth pursuing. I Corinthians 15:58 says, " Therefore, my beloved brethren, be steadfast, immovable, always abounding in the work of the Lord, knowing that your toil is not in vain in the Lord." Further encouragement is found in John 4:36, "Already he who reaps is receiving wages and is gathering fruit for life eternal." When we sow to the Spirit we reap life. So, we don't want to sow to the flesh. You reap what you sow.

Isaiah says in Isaiah 40:31, "Those who wait for the Lord will gain new strength; they will mount up with wings like eagles, they will run and not get tired; they will walk and not become weary."

Don't grow weary. You know the seeds you plant in the ground are working even though you can't see them. If you get impatient and dig them up too soon, you will miss the flowering; you will miss the reaping. Be patient with yourself. God is working even when you can't see it.

To do: Read II Timothy 4

Repeat the memory verse several times today & repeat the first 11 weeks memory verses

Smile for the day: Venison for dinner again. Oh deer.

Week 12 Day 6 Review your memory verse. Record thoughts from this week's devotions and / or prayer requests.

_____
_____
_____
_____
_____
_____
_____
_____
_____
_____
_____
_____
_____
_____
_____
_____
_____
_____
_____
_____
_____
_____
_____
_____
_____

Week 12 Day 7 Review your memory verse. When we pray our prayers should include thanksgiving. Record here what you are thankful for today. Philippians 4:6 "Be anxious for nothing, but in everything by prayer and supplication with thanksgiving let your requests be made known to God."

_____
_____
_____
_____
_____
_____
_____
_____
_____
_____
_____
_____
_____
_____
_____
_____
_____
_____
_____
_____
_____
_____
_____
_____

Week 13 Day 1 <u>Memory verse:</u> "My presence SHALL go with you and I WILL give you rest." Exodus 33:14

<u>MOSES</u>

When I read this verse I think of Moses and how the Lord's presence was always with him as he led the Israelites out of Egypt. Scripture also tells us that Moses not only felt the Lord's presence but they communicated. Whenever Moses would enter the tent (tent of meeting set up outside of camp), the pillar of cloud would descend and stand at the entrance of the tent; and the Lord would speak with Moses. And, in verse 11, "Thus the Lord used to speak to Moses face to face, just as a man speaks to his friend."

Exodus 33 is all about the Lord telling Moses to take the people and depart to the land flowing with milk and honey. But, the Lord says He would not go in their midst because they are an obstinate people. In the end, the Lord does promise Moses He will go with them. But, there's a warning here about the Lord's presence and obstinance. Remember, we are the followers and He is the leader. Let's not let obstinance keep the Lord's presence away from us.

To do: Read Exodus 33

Repeat the memory verse several times today & repeat the first 12 weeks memory verses

Smile of the day: A fine is a tax for doing wrong. A tax is a fine for doing well.

Week 13 Day 2 <u>Memory verse:</u> "My presence SHALL go with you and I WILL give you rest." Exodus 33:14

UPRIGHT

Who shall dwell in God's presence? Psalm 140:13 says, "Surely the righteous will give thanks to your name; the upright will dwell in Your presence." Upright means honest and just. One example of an upright man was Job. "There was a man in the land of Uz whose name was Job; and that man was blameless, upright, fearing God and turning away from evil." (Job 1:1) Noah was another example of an upright man. "Noah was a righteous man, blameless in his time; Noah walked with God." (Genesis 6:9) and Genesis 7:1 says, "Then the Lord said to Noah, 'enter the ark, you and all your household, for you alone I have seen to be righteous before me in this time.'"

One of the most vivid Biblical pictures of God's presence is with Shadrach, Meshach and Abed-nego when they were put in the firey furnace for not worshiping the golden image. They refused knowing they would be put in the furnace and they said to king Nebuchadnezzar "If it be so, our God whom we serve is able to deliver us from the furnace of blazing fire; and He will deliver us out of your hand, O king." (Daniel 3:17) They were bound and put into the furnace and God's presence was with them. The king said , "Look, I see four men loosed and walking about in the midst of the fire without harm, and the appearance of the fourth is like a son of the gods." (verse 25)

To do: Read Daniel 3
           Repeat the memory verse several times today & repeat the first 12 weeks memory verses

Smile for the day: I just got lost in thought. It was unfamiliar territory

FEELING

How do we feel God's presence? There's a difference between knowing and feeling. Knowing is your mind accepting information - I know the Lord loves me. Feeling is absorbing the knowledge -

I feel God's love. You know that the Holy Spirit is with you constantly. Do you feel that? The Spirit helps our weakness; for we do not know how to pray as we should, "but the Spirit Himself intercedes for us with groanings too deep for words." (Romans 8:26) So, one of the things we can do to feel God's presence is to pray. "With all prayer and petition pray at all times in the Spirit" (Ephesians 6:18). (1) So, pray throughout the day. Pray, knowing and feeling that He loves you.

Some other ideas to feel God's presence are: (2) be in the Word daily, absorbing it, not just reading it. You might even want to read scripture out loud. (3) Sing a song, a favorite hymn or praise song when you want to feel God's presence. (3) Out loud, find times throughout the day to say, "Jesus thank you for being with me." (4) Ask the Lord to search your heart and show you any wicked way or sin which you need to confess. Paul's blessing to the Corinthians, "the grace of the Lord Jesus Christ, and the love of God, and the fellowship of the Holy Spirit, be with you all." (II Corinthians 13:14)

To do: Read II Corinthians 13

Repeat the memory verse several times today & repeat the first 12 weeks memory verses

Smile for the day: Honk if you love peace and quiet.

Week 13 Day 4 <u>Memory verse:</u> "My presence SHALL go with you and I WILL give you rest." Exodus 33:14

<u>REST</u>

Joshua loved the Lord. He served Moses and, therefore, was well trained in leadership. Many times in the book of Joshua the Lord promises rest for the Israelites from their enemies. One is Joshua 1:13: "Remember the word which Moses the servant of the Lord commanded you, saying, 'The Lord your God gives you rest and will give you this land." Jeremiah 31:25 says, "For I satisfy the weary ones and refresh everyone who languishes." Matthew 11:28 says, "Come to Me, all who are weary and heavy-laden, and I will give you rest."

What things could cause us to be weary and heavy-laden – sin, anxiety, fear, suffering and afflictions, wrong priorities, business, over-committed, etc. These things cause us to take our focus off of the Lord. If fear is causing you to be weary, notice in Joshua 1:6-9 how God addresses fear to Joshua. He encourages Joshua to be strong and courageous. And David is encouraging Solomon in I Chronicles 22:13 saying, " Be strong and courageous, do not fear nor be dismayed." Remember, one of the reasons we're memorizing scripture is to plant the word of God in our minds and hearts. This will help us to be strong and courageous. The word of God can give us rest.

To do: Read Joshua 1

Repeat the memory verse several times today & repeat the first 12 weeks memory verses

Smile for the day: Change is inevitable, except from a vending machine

Week 13 Day 5 <u>Memory verse:</u> "My presence SHALL go with you and I WILL give you rest." Exodus 33:14

So, let's do a review of this week and what we can do to feel God's presence.

1. Acknowledge His presence daily
2. Pray daily – prayer is two way communication
3. Be in the word daily – absorbing it, not just reading it
4. Sing hymns and songs - sing along with Christian CD's
5. Be strong and courageous – think of Daniel in the lion's den
6. Strive to live righteously – be honest and just
7. Ask for the Lord's guidance daily – part of praying

Most of all, for all of the above to work for you, you need to have faith and trust in the promise given. BELIEVE, God's presence shall go with you. Repeat this to yourself until you start to believe it. Let the faith warriors of the Bible be your examples to follow: Noah, Moses, Paul, the disciples, David, Daniel, etc. I love playing hymns on the piano and singing hymns. The words to "Trust and Obey" reinforce this promise: "When we walk with the Lord in the light of His word, what a glory He sheds on our way! While we do His good will, He abides with us still, and with all who will trust and obey."

To do: Repeat the memory verse several times today & repeat the first 12 weeks memory verses

Smile for the day: Everyone has a photographic memory. Some just don't have film

Week 13 Day 6 Review your memory verse. Record thoughts from this week's devotions and / or prayer requests.

_____
_____
_____
_____
_____
_____
_____
_____
_____
_____
_____
_____
_____
_____
_____
_____
_____
_____
_____
_____
_____
_____
_____
_____
_____
_____

Week 13 Day 7 Review your memory verse. When we pray our prayers should include thanksgiving. Record here what you are thankful for today. Philippians 4:6 "Be anxious for nothing, but in everything by prayer and supplication with thanksgiving let your requests be made known to God."

_____
_____
_____
_____
_____
_____
_____
_____
_____
_____
_____
_____
_____
_____
_____
_____
_____
_____
_____
_____
_____
_____
_____
_____
_____

KAY BRYANT

Week 14 Day 1 Memory verse: "Nor height, nor depth, nor any created thing, WILL be able to separate us from the love of God." Romans 8:39

SEPARATE

Romans 8:35 speaks of created things that cannot separate us from the love of God, "Who will separate us from the love of Christ? Will tribulation, or distress, or persecution, or famine, or nakedness, or peril, or sword?" The rest of verse 39 tells us that the love of God is in Christ Jesus our lord. Romans 8:38 speaks of the other things that cannot separate us from the love of God: "neither death, nor life, nor angels, nor principalities, nor things present, nor things to come, nor powers."

Romans 5:5 says, "hope does not disappoint, because the love of God has been poured out within our hearts through the Holy Spirit who was given to us." Romans 8:16 says, "the Spirit Himself testifies with our spirit that we are children of God." Romans 8 is a great chapter to read about the law of the Spirit of life in Christ Jesus within us. How great is the love of God.

To do: Read Romans 8

Repeat the memory verse several times today & repeat the first 13 weeks memory verses

Smile for the day: If the shoe fits, get another one just like it.

<u>GRACE</u>

Ephesians 2:4-5 says, "But God, being rich in mercy, because of His great love which He loved us, even when we were dead in our transgressions, made us alive together with Christ (by grace you have been saved)." Ephesians 2:8-9 reinforces this saved by grace by adding, "by grace you have been saved through faith; and that not of yourselves, it is the gift of God; not as a result of works, so that no one may boast." Grace is receiving something we don't deserve by God's unmerited favor.

Titus 3:5-6 speaks about how He didn't save us "on the basis of deeds which we have done in righteousnes, but according to His mercy, by the washing of regeneration and renewing by the Holy Spirit, whom He poured out upon us richly through Jesus Christ, our Savior." II Thessalonians 2:16-17 Paul gives a blessing: " Now may our Lord Jesus Christ Himself and God our Father, who has loved us and given us eternal comfort and good hope by grace, comfort and strengthen your hearts in every good work."

To do: Read Ephesians 2

Repeat the memory verse several times today & repeat the first 13 weeks memory verses

Smile for the day: Just remember if it wasn't for gravity, we'd all fall off

Week 14 Day 3 <u>Memory verse:</u> "Nor height, nor depth, nor any created thing WILL be able to separate us from the love of God." Romans 8:39

<u>GOD IS LOVE</u>

I John 4 is a great "Love Chapter." It speaks repeatedly of God's love for us and tells us how we will know of this love. I John 4:7 says, "beloved let us love one another, for love is from God; and everyone who loves is born of God and knows God." I John 4:10 says, "In this is love, not that we loved God, but that He loved us and sent His Son to be the propitiation for our sins." And I John 4:16 says, "We have come to know and have believed the love which God has for us. God is love, and the one who abides in love abides in God, and God abides in him."

When I read these verses I think of missionaries out in the field here in the United States or overseas. I think of their passion, their commitment, their willingness to learn another language if necessary, and raising a family in an unfamiliar environment. They have no idea what their reception will be, what kind of education their children will receive, what kind of challenges they might face on a daily basis. But, these missionaries obviously feel the love of God or they would not be going out there to share that with others. We are called to be missionaries also, to spread the gospel about the love of God right where we are.

To do: Read I John 4
Repeat the memory verse several times today & repeat the first 13 weeks memory verses

Smile for the day: The shin bone is a device for finding furniture

Week 14 Day 4 <u>Memory verse:</u> "Nor height, depth, nor any created thing WILL be able to separate us from the love of God." Romans 8:39

LOVINGKINDNESS

My husband and I are blessed to live at 6000 feet in a high desert area of California where we have awesome views of God's creation every day, sometimes spectacular as we look at distant mountains. So, I thank God for His creation, because it is so vivid where we live. In the midst of a busy city, sometimes it's difficult to see the beauty of the world around you that God created, a beauty that causes us to reflect on His great love. Psalm 136:26 says, "give thanks to the God of heaven for His lovingkindness is everlasting." Psalm 36:5 says, "Your lovingkindness, O Lord, extends to the heavens, Your faithfulness reaches the skies." Psalm 136 is all about God's everlasting lovingkindness.

So, if we go to the highest mountain or to a lowly beach, the height, nor depth can separate us from the love of God. We can't get away from God's love. It's always with us and it's everlasting. No matter what we're going through, be it success or failure, a high point or a low point in our life, nothing can separate us from God's love.

To do: Read Psalm 136

Repeat the memory verse several times today & repeat the first 13 weeks memory verses

Smile for the day: She's always late. In fact, her ancestors arrived on the "Juneflower."

KAY BRYANT

Week 14 Day 5 <u>Memory verse:</u> "Nor height, depth, nor any created thing, WILL be able to separate us from the love of God." Romans 8:39

<u>THIS I KNOW</u>

Let's end today with one of the most favorite hymns of all times which many of us learned as a child. Anna and Susan Warner, after the panic of 1837, started writing poems and songs to supplement the family income. One of their most successful joint projects was a novel titled "Say & Seal" in which a little boy named Johnny Fox was dying. His Sunday School teacher, John Linden, comforts him by taking him in his arms, rocking him, and making up a little song: "Jesus loves me this I know." The novel became a best seller, second only to Uncle Tom's Cabin. When hymnwriter William Bradbury read the words, he composed a childlike musical score to go along with them. "Jesus Loves Me" soon became the best-known children's hymn on earth.

Jesus loves me this I know
For the Bible tells me so
Little ones to Him belong
They are weak but He is strong.

Refrain: Yes, Jesus loves me,
Yes, Jesus loves me,
Yes, Jesus loves me
The Bible tells me so.

Jesus loves me! He will stay,
Close beside me all the way;
He's prepared a home for me,
And, someday His face I'll see

To do: Repeat the memory verse several times today & repeat the first 13 weeks memory verses.

Smile for the day: I wished the buck stopped here, as I could use a few.

Week 14 Day 6 Review your memory verse. Record thoughts from this week's devotions and / or prayer requests.

Week 14 Day 7 Review your memory verse. When we pray our prayers should include thanksgiving. Record here what you are thankful for today. Philippians 4:6 "Be anxious for nothing, but in everything by prayer and supplication with thanksgiving let your requests be made known to God."

_____

_____

_____

_____

_____

_____

_____

_____

_____

_____

_____

_____

_____

_____

_____

_____

_____

_____

_____

_____

Week 15 Day 1 <u>Memory verse:</u> "Only believe that He who began a good work in you WILL perfect it until the day of Jesus Christ." Philippians 1:6

<u>BELIEVE</u>

In Philippians 1, Paul is speaking about standing firm in one Spirit. Paul knew that he was appointed for the defense of the gospel. (verse 16) Therefore, he says in verse 25, "I know that I will remain and continue with you all for your progress and joy in the faith." Paul is the perfect example of believing and pursuing wholeheartedly the work Jesus has given him. In verse 20 he speaks of his "earnest expectation and hope to not be put to shame in anything, but that with all boldness, Christ would be exalted in his body." Verse 21 is one of my all time favorites about Paul: "For me to live is Christ and to die is gain." Paul was a great encourager for people to progress and have joy in their faith. And, he challenges these Christians to "conduct yourselves in a manner worthy of the gospel of Christ, so that whether I come and see you or remain absent, I will hear of you that you are standing firm in one spirit, with one mind striving together for the faith of the gospel." (vs 27)

To do: Read Philippians 1
Repeat the memory verse several times today & repeat the first 14 weeks memory verses

Smile for the day: light travels faster than sound. This is why some people appear bright until you hear them speak.

Week 15 Day 2   <u>Memory verse:</u> "Only believe that He who began a good work in you WILL perfect it until the day of Jesus Christ." Philippians 1:6

PREDESTINED

When did God begin to work in our lives? He knew us before we were born. Psalm 139:16 says, "Your eyes have seen my unformed substance; and in Your book were all written the days that were ordained for me, when as yet there was not one of them." Psalm 139:13-14 says, "For You formed my inward parts; You wove me in my mother's womb. I will give thanks to you for I am fearfully and wonderfully made." And, Ephesians 1:4-5 says, " He (God) chose us in Him before the foundation of the earth, that we would be holy and blameless before Him. In love, He predestined us to adoption as sons through Jesus Christ to Himself, according to the kind intention of His will."

In relation to good works, we have Ephesians 2:10: "For we are His workmanship, created in Christ Jesus for good works which God prepared beforehand so that we would walk in them."

To do: Read Psalm 139

Repeat the memory verse several times today & repeat the first 14 weeks memory verses

Smile for the day: Despite the cost of living, have you noticed how it remains so popular?

Week 15 Day 3 <u>Memory verse:</u> "Only believe that He who began a good work in you WILL perfect it until the day of Jesus Christ." Philippians 1:6

<u>THE BEST</u>

How does God work in our lives? "God is at work in you both to will and to work for his good pleasure." (Philippians 2:13) We need to know, believe "that God causes all things to work together for good to those who love God." (Romans 8:28) And, Proverbs 3:6 says, "In all your ways acknowledge Him, and He will make your paths straight." So, you need to "commit your works to the Lord and your plans will be established." (Proverbs 16:3) Colossians 3:23 says, "Whatever you do, do your work heartily, as for the Lord, rather than for men." I remember learning, at a young age, that whatever my job would be, that I was to do it for the Lord, give it my all, go above and beyond what might be expected of me, beyond the job requirements. I was blessed over the years with a wonderful and varied career in Education with that as my goal.

So, we need to (1) believe God causes all things to work together; (2) in all our ways acknowledge Him; (3) commit our works to the Lord. And, remember while "the mind of man plans his way, the Lord directs his steps." (Proverbs 16:9) Pray about every job you have, including praying about your relations with family members. Strive to be the best mom, the best grandparent, the best sibling, the best son/ daughter possible.

To do: Read Philippians 2

Repeat the memory verse several times today & repeat the first 14 weeks memory verses

Smile for the day: It was recently discovered that research causes cancer in rats

KAY BRYANT

Week 15 Day 4 <u>Memory verse:</u> "Only believe that He who began a good work in you WILL perfect it until the day of Jesus Christ." Philippians 1:6

<u>YOUR WORK</u>

God has also predestined us to do His good works. Each of us has received a spiritual gift and "there are variety of gifts, but the same Spirit; variety of ministries, but the same Lord, varieties of effects, but the same God." (I Corinthians 12:4-6) Whatever your gift, it's for the common good. In your church it's to help build the body of Christ. In the community, your gift is a vehicle for witnessing. Some of the gifts are: wisdom, knowledge, pastors, teachers, leadership, administration, helps, music/worship, faith and prayer warriors. And, I Corinthians goes on to say how each gift is needed to build up the body of the church, by all gifts working together. He compares this to the human body. "If the foot says, 'because I am not an eye, I am not a part of the body,' it is not for this reason any the less a part of the body." (verse 15) It takes all members, utilizing their gifts, to make the body whole.

Titus 2:7,8 says, "In all things show yourself to be an example of good deeds..sound in speech which is beyond reproach, so the opponent will be put to shame, having nothing bad to say about us."

To do: Read I Corinthians 12
Repeat the memory verse several times today & repeat the first 14 weeks memory verses

Smile for the day: Need an ark to save two of every animal? I Noah guy

FAITH AND WORKS

Our work for the Lord should be a vital part of our lives. It needs to be something used, not buried. James 2:17 says, "Even so faith, if it has no works, is dead, being by itself." And, in verse 24, "a man is justified by works and not by faith alone." In verse 18, he continues with "but someone may well say, you have faith and I have works; show me your faith without works, and I will show you my faith by my works." "Just as the body without the spirit is dead, so also faith without works is dead." (verse 26)

So, what is the day of Jesus Christ? This is referring to the blessing and reward for the church at the rapture. When Jesus comes, we want the King to say, "come you who are blessed by My Father, inherit the kingdom prepared for you from the foundation of the world." (Matthew 25:34) So, I look forward with hope to the Day of Christ when "the Lord will rescue me from every evil deed, and will bring me safely to His heavenly kingdom; to Him be the glory forever and ever." (II Timothy 4:18)

To do: Read James 2
　　　　Repeat the memory verse several times today & repeat the first 14 weeks memory verses

Smile for the day: Atheism is a non-prophet organization

Week 15 Day 6 Review your memory verse. Record thoughts from this week's devotions and / or prayer requests.

_____
_____
_____
_____
_____
_____
_____
_____
_____
_____
_____
_____
_____
_____
_____
_____
_____
_____
_____
_____
_____
_____
_____
_____
_____
_____
_____
_____

Week 15 Day 7 Review your memory verse. When we pray our prayers should include thanksgiving. Record here what you are thankful for today. Philippians 4:6 "Be anxious for nothing, but in everything by prayer and supplication with thanksgiving let your requests be made known to God."

_____

_____

_____

_____

_____

_____

_____

_____

_____

_____

_____

_____

_____

_____

_____

_____

_____

_____

_____

_____

_____

_____

_____

KAY BRYANT

Week 16 Day 1 <u>Memory verse:</u> "Peace I leave with you; My peace I GIVE to you; not as the world gives do I GIVE to you." John 14:27

<u>COMFORT</u>

What is peace? Peace is calmness, tranquillity, feeling secure, freedom from disquieting thoughts or emotions and comfort. Comfort gives strength and hope. II Corinthians 1:3,4 says, "Blessed be the God and Father of our Lord Jesus Christ, the Father of mercies and God of all comfort." Romans 5:1 says, " Therefore, having been justified by faith, we have peace with God through our Lord Jesus Christ." In John 14:19,20 Jesus is telling His disciples what is to come: "After a little while the world will no longer see Me, but you will see Me; because I live, you will live also. In that day you will know that I am in My Father, and you in Me and I in you." Both of the promises of John 14 are comforting and peaceful thoughts. John finishes in verse 27b by saying, "do not let your heart be troubled, nor let it be fearful." A troubled heart and fear are two things that will keep you from having peace.

After His resurrection, when He first appeared to the 11 disciples, the first thing He said to them was, "Peace be with you." (John 20:19) And, He repeated that again in verse 21: "Peace be with you; as the Father has sent Me, I also send you." This is a reminder. We spoke of this verse in Week 11.

To do: Read John 14
Repeat the memory verse several times today & repeat the first 15 weeks memory verses

Smile for the day: The meaning of opaque is unclear

THANKFUL

The peace God give us "surpasses all comprehension, and will guard our hearts and minds in Christ Jesus." (Philippians 4:7) We may not comprehend God's peace but we have an inner sense of calm when we receive it. "<u>Let the peace of Christ rule in your hearts,</u> to which indeed you were called in one body; and be thankful." (Colossians 3:15) Our thankfulness then leads to a more positive outlook rather than a negative one. Peace, therefore, is an upward spiral of positive thoughts and emotions. The lack of peace can be a downward spiral leading to negative thoughts and emotions.

Being thankful can help us feel God's peace. "<u>Let the word of Christ richly dwell within you,</u> with all wisdom, teaching and admonishing one another with psalms and hymns and spiritual songs, singing with thankfulness in your hearts to God." (Colossians 3:16) Singing with thankfulness is a joyful and peaceful practice. So, "<u>whatever you do in word or deed,</u> do all in the name of the Lord Jesus, giving thanks through Him to God the Father."(Colossians 3:17)

To do: Read Colossians 3

Repeat the memory verse several times today & repeat the first 15 weeks memory verses

Smile for the day: There was a big paddle sale at the boat store. It was quite and oar deal.

Week 16 Day 3 <u>Memory verse:</u> "Peace I leave with you; My peace I GIVE to you; not as the world gives do I GIVE to you." John 14:27

PURSUE

Yes, the Lord gives us peace, but we are also asked to pursue it. One reason is in Romans 14:19 which says, "we pursue the things which make for peace and the building up of one another." We are called to build up one another in the body of believers. As Ist Corinthians 14:26 says, "When you assemble, each one has a psalm, has a teaching, has a revelation, has an interpretation. Let all things be done for edification." Psalm 34:14 says, "Depart from evil and do good; seek peace and pursue it." II Timothy 2:22 says, " Now flee from youthful lusts and pursue righteousness, faith, love and peace, with those who call on the Lord from a pure heart."

"Pursue peace with all men." (Hebrews 12:14a) Remember in Matthew 5, one of the Beatitudes is: "Blessed are the peacemakers for they shall be called sons of God." (verse 9) Who are the sons of God? "For all who are being led by the Spirit of God, these are sons of God." (Romans 8:14)

To do: Read II Timothy 2

Repeat the memory verse several times today & repeat the first 15 weeks memory verses

Smile for the day: Did you know they won't be making yardsticks any longer?

Week 16 Day 4 <u>Memory verse:</u> "Peace I leave with you; My peace I
GIVE to you; not as the world gives
do I GIVE to you." John 14:27

<u>COVENANT</u>

The Lord, speaking through Isaiah says in Isaiah 54:10, "For the
mountains may be removed and the hills may shake, but my lovingkindness will not be removed from you, and my covenant of peace will
not be shaken." A covenant is a solemn and binding agreement and
there's more than one covenant in the Bible. The first one is promised
to Abraham in Genesis 17:7 where the Lord promises an everlasting
covenant between Himself and Abraham and his descendants saying
that He will be God to all of them. Jeremiah 32:40 says, " I will make
an everlasting covenant with them that I will not turn away from them."

The Lord speaks prophetically in Ezekiel 37:22,24 about what He
will do when David is King saying there will no longer be two kingdoms for Daivd will be the King of all of them. And adds, "I will make
a covenant of peace with them; it will be an everlasting covenant with
them." (verse 26) So, we are assured with a covenant of peace that we
have a solemn and binding agreement on this topic from God. Isaiah
54 is about the heritage for the servants of the Lord, of which peace is
one.

To do: Read Isaiah 54

Repeat the memory verse several times today & repeat the first
15 weeks memory verses

Smile for the day: I used to have a fear of hurdles, but I got over it

Week 16 Day 5 <u>Memory verse:</u> "Peace I leave with you. My peace I GIVE to you; not as the world gives do I GIVE to you." John 14:27

<u>BENEFITS</u>

The word peace appears 100 times in the New Testament. What are the benefits to us from receiving God's gift of peace?

1. God grants us peace in all circumstances (II Thessalonians 3:16)
2. Peace of God rules in our hearts (Colossians 3:15) Be thankful
3. Trust God and He will keep you in perfect peace. (Isaiah 26:3)
4. All of wisdom's paths are peace (Proverbs 3:17)
5. The steadfast of mind He will keep in perfect peace. (Isaiah 25:3)

A prophecy from Isaiah 9:6 says, " For a child will be born to us, a son will be given to us; and the government will rest on His shoulders; and His name will be called Wonderful Counselor, Mighty God, Eternal Father, Prince of Peace." What kind of peace does the world give us? Well, agreements aren't always binding and frequently broken and not everlasting. That's why we have wars, divorces, adultery, murders, job loss, selfish ambitions, etc. "Wisdom's ways are pleasant and all her paths are peace." (Proverbs 3:17) Proverbs 3 shares a lot of thoughts on how wisdom leads to peace.

To do: Read Proverbs 3
        Repeat the memory verse several times today & repeat the first 15 weeks memory verses

Smile for the day: I'm reading a book about anti-gravity. I can't put it down

Week 16 Day 6 Review your memory verse. Record thoughts from this week's devotions and / or prayer requests.

_____

_____

_____

_____

_____

_____

_____

_____

_____

_____

_____

_____

_____

_____

_____

_____

_____

_____

_____

_____

_____

_____

_____

_____

Week 16 Day 7 Review your memory verse. When we pray our prayers should include thanksgiving. Record here what you are thankful for today. Philippians 4:6 "Be anxious for nothing, but in everything by prayer and supplication with thanksgiving let your requests be made known to God."

_____
_____
_____
_____
_____
_____
_____
_____
_____
_____
_____
_____
_____
_____
_____
_____
_____
_____
_____
_____
_____
_____
_____
_____

Week 17 Day 1 <u>Memory verse:</u> **"Quick to hear, slow to speak and slow to anger for this is God's WILL." James 1:19**

<u>HEARERS AND DOERS</u>

Quick is defined as: fast in understanding, thinking or learning; aroused immediately and intensely. So what are we to be quick to hear? Jesus spoke many parables to the crowds and frequently ended with, "He who has ears to hear, let him hear." (Mark 4:9) A parable is a story told that paints a picture and helps to make a point. In Mark 4:12 Jesus says that those who are unbelievers "while seeing, they may see and not perceive, and while hearing, they may hear and and not understand." But, "Jesus was explaining everything privately to His own disciples." (Mark 4:34)

James 1:22 says, "But prove yourselves doers of the word, and not merely hearers who delude themselves." Romans 2:13 adds to this thought by saying, " for it is not the hearers of the Law who are just before God, but the doers of the Law will be justified." James 1:25 says, " But one who looks intently at the perfect law, the law of liberty, and abides by it, not having become a forgetful hearer but an effectual doer, this man will be blessed in what he does."

To do: Read James 1

Repeat the memory verse several times today & repeat the first 16 weeks memory verses

Smile for the day: Police were called to a day care center. A 3-year old was resisting a rest.

Week 17 Day 2 <u>Memory verse:</u> "Quick to hear, slow to speak and slow to anger for this is God's WILL." James 1:19

POWER

James 3 is all about the power of the tongue and the blessing and damage it can do. Verse 5a says, " the tongue is a small part of the body, and yet it boasts of great things." Verse 6 says, "And the tongue is a fire, the very world of iniquity; the tongue is set among our members as that which defiles the entire body, and sets on fire the course of our life and is set on fire by hell." Verses 8,10 say, "No one can tame the tongue; it is a restless evil and full of deadly poison. From the same mouth come both blessing and cursing. My brethren, things ought not to be this way."

Psalm 140:3 says, evil men, "sharpen their tongues as a serpent; poison of a viper is under their lips." Proverbs 18:21 says, "death and life are in the power of the tongue." So, we need to always be aware of the power of our words to bring a blessing and bring a hurt. Proverbs 16:24 gives good advice: "Pleasant words are a honeycomb, sweet to the soul and healing to the bones." So being slow to anger is great advice. I also think, taking a deep breath and praying about what to say is good advice. Remember God is always with you and always a protector.

To do: Read James 3
Repeat the memory verse several times today & repeat the first 16 weeks memory verses

Smile for the day: A relief map shows where the restrooms are

Week 17 Day 3 <u>Memory verse:</u> "**Quick to hear, slow to speak and slow to anger for this is God's WILL.**" James 1:19

<u>ON GUARD</u>

Now that we've reviewed the power of the tongue, we suddenly feel a little intimidated. What else do we need to know about the power of the tongue?

1. The heart of the wise instructs his mouth & adds persuasiveness to his lips. (Prov 16:23)
2. By your words you will be justified, & by your words you'll be condemned (Matt 12:37)
3. Do not lie to one another, since you laid aside the old self (Colossians 3:9)
4. Whatever you do in word or deed, do all in the name of the Lord Jesus (Col 3:17)
5. One who guards his mouth preserves his life. (Proverbs 13:3)
6. He who guards his mouth & his tongue guards his soul from trouble. (Proverbs 21:23)
7. Let your speech always be with grace, as though seasoned with salt (Col 4:6)
8. He who restrains his words has knowledge. (Proverbs 17:27)

And, finally, James 5:12 says, "But above all, my brethren, do not swear, either by heaven or by earth or with any other oath; but your yes is to be yes, and your no, no, so that you may not fall under judgment." "Pleasant words are a honeycomb, sweet to the soul and healing to the bones."(Prov 16:24)

To do: Read Proverbs 16
Repeat the memory verse several times today and repeat the first 16 weeks memory verses

Smile for the day: Flashlight - a case for holding dead batteries

KAY BRYANT

Week 17 Day 4 <u>Memory verse:</u> "Quick to hear, slow to speak and slow to anger for this is God's WILL." James 1:19

<u>USE DISCRETION</u>

You know slow is the opposite of quick. So, what does scripture have to say about being slow to anger?

1. He who is slow to anger is better than the mighty (Proverbs 16:32)
2. Be angry and do not sin; do not let the sun go down on your anger. (Ephesians 4:26)
3. He who is slow to anger has great understanding. (Proverbs 14:29)
4. A quick tempered man acts foolishly (Proverbs 14:17)
5. A man's discretion makes him slow to anger. (Proverbs 19:11)
6. A man of great anger will bear the penalty (Proverbs 19:19)
7. Do not be eager in your heart to be angry for anger resides in the bosom of the fool (Ecclesiastes 7:9)

To do: Read Proverbs 19
Repeat the memory verse several times today & repeat the first 16 weeks memory verses

Smile for the day: The other day I held a door open for a clown. I thought it was a nice jester.

Week 17 Day 5 <u>Memory verse:</u> "Quick to hear, slow to speak and slow to anger for this is God's WILL." James 1:19

<u>GOD'S WILL</u>

What is God's will? A general response is that God's will is <u>His teachings for all people</u>. We know that God "desires all men to be saved and to come to the <u>knowledge of the truth</u>" (I Timothy 2:4) When we say the Lord's Prayer in Matthew 6:10 we speak of God's will: "Your kingdom come, Your will be done on earth as it is in heaven." Romans 12:2 indicates what that might be in heaven: "do not be conformed to this world, but be transformed by the renewing of your mind, so that you may prove what the will of God is, that which is <u>good,</u> and <u>acceptable</u> and <u>perfect.</u>"

Paul is praying for believers in Colossians 1:9 saying, "we have not ceased to pray for you and to ask that you may be filled with the knowledge of His will in all <u>spiritual wisdom</u> and <u>understanding</u>." So, our goal is "to <u>rejoice always; pray without ceasing; in everything give thanks;</u> for this is God's will for you in Christ Jesus." (I Thessalonians 5:16-18). So, if we are going to renew our minds and be filled with knowledge of His will we need to be in the word, daily.

To do: Read I Thessalonians 5
    Repeat the memory verse several times today & repeat the first 16 weeks memory verses

Smile for the day: My tailor is happy to make a new pair of pants for me. Or sew it seams

Week 17 Day 6 Review your memory verse. Record thoughts from this week's devotions and / or prayer requests.

_____
_____
_____
_____
_____
_____
_____
_____
_____
_____
_____
_____
_____
_____
_____
_____
_____
_____
_____
_____
_____
_____
_____
_____
_____
_____
_____

Week 17 Day 7 Review your memory verse. When we pray our prayers should include thanksgiving. Record here what you are thankful for today. Philippians 4:6 "Be anxious for nothing, but in everything by prayer and supplication with thanksgiving let your requests be made known to God."

_____
_____
_____
_____
_____
_____
_____
_____
_____
_____
_____
_____
_____
_____
_____
_____
_____
_____
_____
_____
_____
_____
_____

KAY BRYANT

Week 18 Day 1 <u>Memory verse:</u> "Remain faithful until death and I WILL give you the crown of life." Revelation 2:10

OVERCOME

To be faithful is to be loyal and trustworthy; to be steadfast in keeping promises or in fulfilling duties. So, how do we remain faithful to God throughout our lives? I John 5:4 says, "for whatever is born of God overcomes the world; and this is the victory that has overcome the world – our faith."

Overcoming is part of the way we can stay faithful. I John 4:4 says, "You are from God and have overcome them (the evil one); because greater is He that is in you than he who is in the world." We pray for and receive God's strength to help us overcome. Romans 12:21 says, "Do not be overcome by evil but overcome evil with good."

Revelation 2 is a message to four churches (Ephesus, Smyrna, Pergamum, Thyatira) commenting on their good and bad points. Verse 7 says, "hear what the Spirit says to the churches, to him who overcomes, I will grant to eat of the tree of life which is in the Paradise of God." Our promise verse above in Revelation 2:10 is preceeded by saying "do not fear what you are about to suffer" as you will be tested.

To do: Read Revelation 2

Repeat the memory verse several times today and repeat the first 17 weeks memory verses

Smile for the day: A day without sunshine is like, well, night.

Week 18 day 2 <u>Memory verse:</u> "Remain faithful until death and I WILL give you the crown of life." Revelation 2:10

<u>JUSTIFY</u>

Romans 5:1 says that, "having been justified by faith, we have peace with God through our Lord Jesus Christ." And, Romans 5:9 says, "having now been justified by His blood, we shall be saved from the wrath of God through Him." There's a promise. And, Romans 3:24 says, "being justified as a gift by His grace through the redemption which is in Christ Jesus." Justify means to declare guiltless. Psalm 31:23 says, "O love the Lord, all you His godly ones! The Lord preserves the faithful." Being faithful to the Lord shows our love for Him. And, "the Lord keeps all who love Him" (Psalm 145:20) Paul says in Romans 8:30, "and these whom He predestined, He also called; and these whom He called, He also justified, and these whom He justified, He also glorified."

Paul is an awesome example of a faithful believer in all circumstances. His life is an example to us of how to remain faithful until death. He tells how the Lord strengthened him because he was faithful in I Timothy 1:12. The Lord will strengthen us also if we are faithful.

To do: Read Romans 5

Repeat the memory verse several times today and repeat the first 17 weeks memory verses

Smile for the day: Laugh every day. It's like inner jogging

KAY BRYANT

Week 18 Day 3 <u>Memory verse:</u> "Remain faithful until death and I WILL give you the crown of life." Revelation 2:10

<u>BY FAITH....</u>

Hebrews 11 is a chronological listing of the "faithful until death" of Old Testament believers.

It's a very inspirational chapter to read. It's like the "Who's Who" of the Old Testament. Hebrews 11 begins in verse 1 saying, " Now faith is the assurance of things hoped for, the conviction of things not seen" It's how the men of old gained approval. Here are some great examples;

1. "By faith, Enoch was taken up so that he would not see death because he was pleasing to God (verse 5)"
2. "By faith Noah being warned by God about things not yet seen, in reverence prepared an ark for the salvation of his family & became an heir of righteousness (verse7)"
3. "By faith, Abraham obeyed God by going out to a place which he was to receive as an inheritance and he went out, not knowing where he was going (verse 8)"
4. "By faith, Sarah, was able to conceive beyond the proper time of life because she considered Him faithful who had promised. (verse 11)"
5. "By faith, Rahab, the harlot did not perish along with those who were disobedient, after she had welcomed the spies in peace. (verse 31)"

This chapter goes on to mention many others and what they accomplished by being faithful.

To do: Read Hebrews 11

Repeat the memory verse several times today and repeat the first 17 weeks memory verses

Smile for the day: Sign on a plumber's truck: "Don't sleep with a drip. Call your plumber"

Week 18 Day 4 <u>Memory verse</u>: "Remain faithful until death and I WILL give you the crown of life." Revelation 2:10

<u>PERSEVERE</u>

What is the crown of life? James 1:12 says, "Blessed is a man who perseveres under trial, for once he has been approved, he will receive the crown of life which the Lord has promised to those who love him." Both the references in Revelation and James speak of faithfulness in persevering under trial. The crown of life is an honor bestowed that will be awarded at the judgement seat of Christ. The crown of life is for all of us who persevere in the faith. The crown of life is another way to say eternal life. Paul speaks of an imperishable (not subject to decay) wreath given for exercising self-control in all things in I Corinthians 9:25. The crown of life is given to all who enter God's kingdom, to those who truly love God and are faithful until death. I Corinthians 9 is a great chapter to read where Paul describes his faith and his motivation. A chapter that should be very inspirational for you.

To do: Read I Corinthians 9

Repeat the memory verse several times today & repeat the first 17 weeks memory verses

Smile for the day: Sign on a Septic Tank Truck: Yesterday's meals on wheels

Week 18 Day 5 <u>Memory verse:</u> "Remain faithful until death and I WILL give you the crown of life." Revelation 2:10

REWARD

When I think of a crown , I visualize a King or a Queen that I've seen pictures of wearing a crown, like Queen Elizabeth or Princess Diana. A crown is for someone who stands out above the rest. It is a royal headdress. A queen in the Old Testament was Esther. King Ahasuerus "loved Esther more than all women and she found favor and kindness with him more than all the virgins, so that he set the royal crown on her head and made her queen." (Esther 2:17). Proverbs 12:4 says, "an excellent wife is the crown of her husband." And, Proverbs 31:11-12 describes an excellent wife: "The heart of her husband trusts in her and she does him good and not evil all the days of her life." God needs to know He can trust us all the days of our life.

So, the crown of life is an honor bestowed on all who truly love God and are faithful until death. Remember, it is a gift to all who enter God's kingdom. You might say the "crown"-ing touch is eternal life.

To do: Read Esther 2

Repeat the memory verse several times today & repeat the first 17 weeks memory verses

Smile for the day: Sign in a Podiatrist's office: "Time wounds all heels"

Week 18 Day 6 Review your memory verse. Record thoughts from this week's devotions and / or prayer requests.

Week 18 Day 7 Review your memory verse. When we pray our prayers should include thanksgiving. Record here what you are thankful for today. Philippians 4:6 "Be anxious for nothing, but in everything by prayer and supplication with thanksgiving let your requests be made known to God."

_____
_____
_____
_____
_____
_____
_____
_____
_____
_____
_____
_____
_____
_____
_____
_____
_____
_____
_____
_____
_____
_____
_____
_____
_____

Week 19 Day 1 <u>Memory verse:</u> "Surely I WILL help you. Surely I WILL uphold you with My righteous right hand." Isaiah 41:10bc

<u>ASSIST</u>

A helper is one who assists. Think of the people throughout your life you have depended upon for help: your parents, your teachers, your doctors, your pastor, your Bible Study teachers, your Pharmacist, your dentist, etc. Most of Isaiah 41 is about what the Lord will do for Israel and how He will help them. He tells them not to fear for He will strengthen and help them. In verse 14 He says, "I will help you and your Redeemer is the Holy One of Israel." He goes on to tell them what they will be able to do because of His help. (verses 8-16) and what He Himself can do (verses 17-20)

All of the helpers mentioned above help us during different periods of our lives. But, God is our Helper throughout our lives. Psalm 48:14 says, "For such is God, Our God forever and ever; He will guide us until death." We have repeated assurance in scripture that He is our helper. Psalm 54:4 says, "Behold, God is my helper; The Lord is the sustainer of my soul."

To do: Read Isaiah 41

Repeat the memory verse several times today and repeat the first 18 weeks memory verses

Smile for the day: A sign on a blinds and curtain truck: "Blind man driving."

Week 19 Day 2 <u>Memory verse:</u> "Surely I WILL help you. Surely I
WILL uphold you with My righteous
right hand." Isaiah 41:10bc

<u>PRAY</u>

If you want God's help, you should pray and ask for it. Psalm 30:10
David says, "Hear, O Lord, and be gracious to me; O Lord, be my
helper." Psalm 27:9 says, "Do not hide your face from me, do not turn
Your servant away in anger; You have been my help; Do not abandon
me nor forsake me, O God of my salvation." In Psalm 27:4 David
shares another prayer: "One thing I have asked from the Lord, that I
shall seek; that I may dwell in the house of the Lord all the days of my
life, to behold the beauty of the Lord." David had total trust that God
was His helper and proclaims this again in Psalm 54:4: "Behold, God
is my helper; the Lord is the sustainer of my soul."

In Luke 18:1, Jesus is telling His disciples "they ought to pray and
not to lose heart." He then tells a parable (verses 2-6) and ends up saying in verse 7, "will not God bring about justice for His elect who cry
to Him day and night, and will He delay long over them?" So, we are
to "pray without ceasing" (I Thessalonians 5:17) because we have the
assurance that God will help us.

To do: Read Psalm 27
Repeat the memory verse several times today & repeat the first
18 weeks memory verses

Smile for the day: At a propane filling station: "Thank Heaven for little
grills."

Week 19 Day 3 <u>Memory verse:</u> "Surely I WILL help you. Surely I WILL uphold you with my righteous right hand." Isaiah 41:10bc

<u>TRUST</u>

We need to trust that the Lord will help us and be our Helper. Psalm 22:4 David says, "In You our fathers trusted; they trusted and You delivered them." In I Chronicles 5:18,19 we read that the sons of Reuben and the Gadites and the half-tribe of Manasseh made war against the Hagrites, Jetur, Naphish and Nodab. Verse 20 says, "They were helped against them, and the Hagrites and all who were with them were given into their hand; for they cried out to God in the battle, and He answered their prayers because they trusted in Him."

II Samuel 8:6 tell us that "the Lord helped David wherever he went." In II Samuel 3:18 the Lord says, "By the hand of My servant David I will save My people Israel from the hand of the Philistines and from the hand of all their enemies." Why? Because David trusted the Lord in all circumstances. Psalm 56:11 says, "In God I have put my trust, I shall not be afraid. What can man do to me?" And Psalm 54:4 says, "Behold, God is my helper; The Lord is the sustainer of my soul." We can all aspire to have the faith and trust in the Lord that David had.

To do: Read Psalm 54

Repeat the memory verse several times today & repeat the first 18 weeks memory verses

Smile for the day: In a Veterinarian's waiting room: "Be back in 5 minutes. Sit! Stay!"

Week 19 Day 4 <u>Memory verse:</u> "Surely I WILL help you. Surely I WILL uphold you with my righteous right hand." Isaiah 41:10bc

MIGHTY HAND

What do we know about God's righeous right hand? Psalm 89:13 says, "You have a strong arm; Your hand is mighty, Your right hand is exalted." Psalm 98:1cd says, "His right hand and His holy arm have gained the victory for Him." Psalm 118:16 says, "The right hand of the Lord is exalted; the right hand of the Lord does valiantly." Exodus 15:6 says, "Your right hand, O Lord, is majestic in power, Your right hand, O Lord, shatters the enemy."

The Lord is speaking to Moses in Exodus 3:20 where He says, "I will stretch out My hand and strike Egypt with all My miracles which I shall do in the midst of it; and after that he will let you go." Isaiah 41:13 says, "For I am the Lord your God, who upholds your right hand, Who says to you, do not fear, I will help you." Interesting, we know the Lord holds our hand from Isaiah 42:6: "I will also hold you by the hand and watch over you." Look at your right hand and remind yourself that the Lord holds it. Exodus 3 is an excellent example of what the Lord does as a helper, what He did for Moses and how He promised to help him.

To do: Read Exodus 3

Repeat the memory verse several times today & repeat the first 18 weeks memory verses

Smile for the day: Outside a Muffler Shop: "No appointment necessary. We hear you coming."

Week 19 Day 5 Memory verse: "Surely I WILL help you. Surely I WILL uphold you with my righteous right hand." Isaiah 41:10bc

RIGHTEOUS

Interesting, most of the references this week were from Psalms. This is a great testimony of how David totally looked upon God as his helper in all circumstances. What are some ways that God helps us? Psalm 32:8 says, "I will instruct you and teach you in the way you should go; I will counsel you with my eye upon you." Proverbs 6:23 says, "For the commandment is a lamp and the teaching is light; and reproofs for discipline are the way of life." I like the analogy of comparing the scriptures that we read as a lamp and a light. These are two things necessary to overcome darkness. And, as we already know, the word is one way God helps us.

Referring to God's hand as righteous is because God is righteousness. Righteousness is a state of moral perfection. A righteous person is a virtuous person. Genesis 6:9 says, "Noah was a righteous man, blameless in his time; Noah walked with God." "The salvation of the righteous is from the Lord; The Lord helps them and delivers them." (Psalm 37:39-40) Three times in the New Testament we are told "the righteous man shall live by faith." (Romans 1:17, Galations 3:11, Hebrews 10:38) Let our faith reflect our belief and trust in the Lord as our helper.

To do: Read Psalm 37

Repeat the memory verse several times today and repeat the first 18 weeks memory verses

Smile for the day: Sign in shoe repair store: "We will heel you, we will save your sole, we will even dye for you."

Week 19 Day 6 Review your memory verse. Record thoughts from this week's devotions and / or prayer requests.

_____

_____

_____

_____

_____

_____

_____

_____

_____

_____

_____

_____

_____

_____

_____

_____

_____

_____

_____

_____

_____

_____

_____

_____

_____

_____

_____

_____

_____

Week 19 Day 7 Review your memory verse. When we pray our prayers should include thanksgiving. Record here what you are thankful for today. Philippians 4:6 "Be anxious for nothing, but in everything by prayer and supplication with thanksgiving let your requests be made known to God."

_____
_____
_____
_____
_____
_____
_____
_____
_____
_____
_____
_____
_____
_____
_____
_____
_____
_____
_____
_____
_____
_____
_____
_____
_____

Week 20 Day 1 <u>Promise verse:</u> "The free gift God WILL give is eternal life in Christ Jesus our Lord." Romans 6:23

<u>THE GIFT</u>

We receive this gift when we become Christians and accept Jesus as our Lord and Savior, affirming His virgin birth, His death and His resurrection for the forgiveness of our sins. And, what is this gift? John 17:3 defines eternal life for us: "This is eternal life, that they may know You, the only true God, and Jesus Christ whom You have sent." This gift tell us that "the one who confesses the Son has the Father also." (I John 2:23) The promised gift is reaffirmed in I John 2:25, " This is the promise which He Himself made to us: eternal life." So, while we receive this gift when we become a Christian, eternal life itself doesn't begin til after the rapture.

Romans 6 is a great chapter to read about the contrast in a life of sin and the newness of life that we walk in with Christ. It speaks of how we believe that our old self was crucified with Him, through the forgiveness of our sins, and now we shall also live with Him. (verses 5,6,8)

To do: Read Romans 6

Repeat the memory verse several times today & repeat the first 19 weeks memory verses

Smile for the day: On an Electrician's truck: "Let us remove your shorts"

<u>EVERLASTING</u>

Perhaps the first Bible verse children memorize in Sunday School is John 3:16, "For God so loved the world that He gave His only be-gotten Son, that whoever believes in Him shall not perish, but have eternal life." That verse pretty much says it all. The meaning of eternal is everlasting. So, we are promised a life that will continue in eternity, whereas those who do not believe in Jesus as their Lord and Savior have a life that ends with death and they go to eternal damnation. (Matthew 25:46) And again, John 3:36 says, "He who believes in the Son has eternal life; but he who does not obey the Son will not see life, but the wrath of God abides on him."

Think about the meaning of everlasting. It's like there is no end. Surely, everyone needs to make a wise decision about where they are going to continue to live forever, eternally. John 3 is a great chapter to read on the importance of being born again. You must be born again to have eternal life, everlasting life. John 3:16 is a promise you should also memorize if you haven't already.

To do: Read John 3

Repeat the memory verse several times today & repeat the first 19 weeks memory verses

Smile for the day: At an Optometrist's Office: "If you don't see what you're looking for, you've come to the right place."

Week 20 Day 3 <u>Memory verse:</u> "The free Gift God WILL give is eternal life in Christ Jesus our Lord." Romans 6:23

<u>MORE</u>

The promise of eternal life also includes more promises. John 5:24 says, "Truly, truly, I say to you, he who hears My word and believes Him who sent Me, has eternal life and does not come into judgment, but has passed out of death into life." And, John 10:28 says, "I give eternal life to them, and they will never perish; and no one will snatch them out of My hand." That's a comforting thought.

John 5:28-29 says, "Do not marvel at this; for an hour is coming, in which all who are in the tombs will hear His voice, and will come forth; those who did the good deeds to a resurrection of life, those who committed the evil deeds to a resurrection of judgment." And, what is promised to the resurrection of the believers for their bodies? (1) "it is sown a perishable body, it is raised an imperishable body; (2) it is sown in dishonor, it is raised in glory; (3) it is sown in weakness, it is raised in power; (4) it is sown a natural body, it is raised a spiritual body." (I Corinthians 15:42-44) And, Matthew 13:43 says, "Then the righteous shall shine forth as the sun in the kingdom of their Father." Lots to look forward to.

To do: Read Matthew 13
        Repeat the memory verse several times today & repeat the first
        19 weeks memory verses

Smile for the day: In the front yard of a funeral home:" Drive carefully. We'll wait"

Week 20 Day 4 <u>Memory verse:</u> "The free gift God WILL give is eternal life in Christ Jesus our Lord." Romans 6:23

<u>BELIEVE</u>

John 6:40 says, "this is the will of my Father, that everyone who beholds the Son and believes in Him will have eternal life." And, verse 47 says, "truly, truly, I say to you, he who believes has eternal life." In John 11:25 Jesus says, "I am the resurrection and the life; he who believes in Me will live even if he dies, and everyone who lives and believes in Me will never die."

John 6 is loaded with scriptural gems like John 6:38-39, "For I have come down from heaven, not to do My own will, but the will of Him who sent Me. This is the will of Him who sent Me, that of all that He has given Me I lose nothing, but raise it up on the last day." John 5:21 says, "As sin reigned in death, even so grace would reign through righteousness to eternal life through Jesus Christ our Lord." Believe, Jesus doesn't want to lose us and wants us to join Him eternally.

To do: Read John 6

Repeat the memory verse several times today and repeat the first 19 weeks memory verses

Smile for the day: Arbitrator: A cook that leaves Arby's to work at McDonalds

Week 20 Day 5 <u>Memory verse:</u> "The free gift God WILL give is eternal life in Christ Jesus our Lord." Romans 6:23

<u>OBEY</u>

Not only are we to believe in Jesus, we are also expected to obey Him. Obeying is part of believing. Hebrews 5:8-9 says, "Although He was a Son, He learned obedience from the things which He suffered. And having been made perfect, He became to all those who obey Him the source of eternal salvation." I John 2:3 says, "By this we know that we have come to know Him, if we keep His commandments." John 14:21a says, "He who has My commandments and keeps them is the one who loves Me," Peter says in Acts 5:29, "We must obey God rather than men."

Samuel says in I Samuel 15:22, " Has the Lord as much delight in burnt offerings and sacrifices, as in obeying the voice of the Lord? Behold, to obey is better than sacrifice, and to heed than the fat of rams." And, Moses speaking to all of Israel says, " You shall therefore obey the Lord Your God, and do His commandments and His statutes which I command you today." (Deuteronomy 27:10) Yes, eternal life is a free gift, but we are to show our thankfulness for that gift by the way we respond: to believe, to love and to obey.

To do: Read I Samuel 15
Repeat the memory verse several times today and repeat the first 19 weeks memory verses

Smile for the day: Avoidable: What a bullfighter tries to do

Week 20 Day 6 Review your memory verse. Record thoughts from this week's devotions and / or prayer requests.

KAY BRYANT

Week 20 Day 7 Review your memory verse. When we pray our prayers should include thanksgiving. Record here what you are thankful for today. Philippians 4:6 "Be anxious for nothing, but in everything by prayer and supplication with thanksgiving let your requests be made known to God."

_____

_____

_____

_____

_____

_____

_____

_____

_____

_____

_____

_____

_____

_____

_____

_____

_____

_____

_____

_____

_____

_____

_____

_____

_____

Week 21 Day 1 <u>Memory verse:</u> "Use the full armor of God so that you WILL be able to stand firm against the devil's schemes." Ephesians 6:11

LOINS: TRUTH

The full armor of God is: (1) gird loins with truth, (2) breastplate of righteousness, (3) shod feet with preparation of the gospel of peace, (4) shield of faith, (5) helmet of salvation and (6) sword of the Spirit. We will address each one of these. The reason we need the full armor of God to resist the devil's schemes is because "our struggle is not against flesh and blood, but against the rulers, against the powers, against the world forces of this darkness, against the spiritual forces of wickedness in the heavenly places." (Ephesians 6:12) Ephesians 6:18 follows the list of pieces of armor by saying to "pray at all times in the Spirit." Faith, prayer and truth are necessary to activate the armor. The armor is what enables us to "be dressed for readiness." (Luke 12:35)

GIRD YOUR LOINS WITH TRUTH (verse 14) Your core (loins) is the central link that connects your upper and lower parts of your body and helps with your balance, stability and stamina. And what holds your core together is truth enabling you to stand firm. To hold on to God's truth, Ist Peter 1:13 says, "Therefore, prepare your minds for action, keep sober in spirit, fix your hope completely on the grace to be brought to you at the revelation of Jesus Christ." We need to be supported with the truth (God's truths) in our decisions to know when, where and how to move.

To do: Read Ephesians 6

Repeat the memory verse several times today and repeat the first 20 weeks memory verses

Smile for the day: ECLIPSE: What an English barber does for a living

BREASTPLATE: RIGHTEOUSNESS

BREASTPLATE OF RIGHTEOUSNESS (verse 14) The breast-plate the Roman soldier wore protected his heart and, without it, would have resulted in certain death. Proverbs 4:23 says, "Watch over your heart with all diligence, for from it flow the springs of life." My heart is the centerpiece of my soul. And, my soul is what makes me a unique person because it encompasses my mind, my will, my emotion and my conscience.

Righteousness is right living. Psalm 119:172 says, "For all your commandments are righteousness." Romans 10:10 says, "for with the heart a person believes, resulting in righteousness, and with the mouth he confesses, resulting in salvation." Psalm 23:3 says, "He restores my soul; He guides me in the paths of righteousness." Our goal is to pursue God's perfect standard of righteousness; of justice and holiness. It's God's righteousness that we put on for protection. Because of Jesus' death and resurrection, God does not see your sin but sees you as a righteous person.

To do: Read Proverbs 11

Repeat the memory verse several times today and repeat the first 20 weeks memory verses

Smile for the day: BURGLARIZE: What a crook sees with

Week 21 Day 3 <u>Memory verse:</u> "Use the full armor of God so that you WILL be able to stand firm against the devil's schemes." Ephesians 6:11

<u>FEET: GOSPEL OF PEACE</u>

SHOD YOUR FEET WITH THE PREPARATION OF THE GOSPEL OF PEACE. (verse 15) Romans 10:15 says, "How beautiful are the feet of those who bring good news of great things." Our shoes move us forward so we can see where we are going. And, we are to bring good news. Isaiah 52:7 says, "How lovely on the mountains are the feet of him who brings good news, who announces peace, and brings good news of happiness, who announces salvation." The crucial part of this piece of armor is that we need peace. Here is an assurance for which we are to be thankful in Romans 5:1, "Since we have been declared righteous by faith, we have peace with God through our Lord Jesus Christ." One reason we need the peace of God is because the devil's top priority is to unsettle us as he doesn't want us to have peace. Paul says in Ephesians 4:1-3, "Therefore I, the prisoner of the Lord, implore you to walk in a manner worthy of the calling with which you have been called, with all humility and gentleness, with patience, showing tolerance for one another in love, being diligent to preseve the unity of the Spirit in the bond of peace."

To do: Read Ephesians 4
  Repeat the memory verse several times today and repeat the first 20 weeks memory verses

Smile for the day: HEROES: What a guy in a boat does

Week 21 Day 4 <u>Memory verse:</u> "Use the full armor of God so that you WILL be able to stand firm against the devil's schemes." Ephesians 6:11

<u>SHIELD: FAITH</u>

SHIELD OF FAITH (verse 16) Verse 16 says with the shield of faith "you will be able to extinguish all the flaming arrows of the evil one." The shield is held up in front of you, in front of all the other pieces of armor you are wearing. Galations 2:20 says, " I have been crucified with Christ; and it is no longer I who live, but Christ lives in me; and the life which I now live in the flesh, I live by faith in the Son of God, who loved me and gave Himself up for me." The devil sends firey arrows to try and distract us in our walk of faith. Remember, faith was defined in Week 18 Day 3.

Think of the people throughout your life that you've had faith in. You totally belileved what they said. You totally believed what they promised to do. Our faith shows what we believe to be true about God. When we walk in our faith without doubt and fear, and with total trust, we can use the shield of faith confidently and securely.

To do: Read Galations 2:20
        Repeat the memory verse several times today and repeat the first 20 weeks memory verses

Smile for the day: PARADOX: Two physicians

Week 21 Day 5 <u>Memory verse:</u> "Use the full armor of God so that you WILL be able to stand firm against the devil's schemes." Ephesians 6:11

HELMET: SALVATION

HELMET OF SALVATION: (verse 17) We know a helmet protects the head. The Roman soldier's helmet was made of iron and protected the head and brain. The brain is where our thoughts are centered. I Thessalonians 5:8 says, " the helmet is the hope of salvation." Salvation is deliverance. And, salvation is obtained "through our Lord Jesus Christ." (I Thessalonians 5:9) What is the connection between helmet and salvation? Without a helmet, your head and your brain are not protected. Without salvation, your mind is not protected. II Corinthians 10:4-5 says, the weapons of our warfare are divinely powerful for the destruction of fortresses. "We are destroying speculations and every lofty thing raised up against the knowledge of God, and we are taking every thought captive to the obedience of Christ." The gospel is the power of God for salvation to everyone who believes (Romans 1:16) Salvation is a protective measure as it controls our thinking. Keep in the word.

SWORD: WORD OF GOD

SWORD OF THE SPIRIT WHICH IS THE WORD OF GOD. (verse 17) The sword of the Spirit is the only defensive weapon. All the other pieces of armor are offensive weapons for protection. Hebrews 4:12 says, "For the word of God is living and active and sharper than any two-edged sword, and piercing as far as the division of soul and spirit, of both joints and marrow, and able to judge the thoughts and intensions of the heart." "Is not My word like fire?" declares the Lord, and "like a hammer which shatters a rock?" (Jeremiah 23:29)

Remember, from the introduction to this book, where it was mentioned that without being able to draw on the word of God, the sword of the Spirit, you have no defense. This is one of the reasons to memorize scripture. This was the motivation for this book. This is the motivation for you adding memory verses to your mind weekly.

The weapons of our warfare are divinely powerful for the destruction of fortresses as "we are destroying speculations and every lofty thing raised up against the knowledge of God, and we are taking every thought captive to the obedience of Christ." (II Corinthians 10:4,5) So, let us put on the full armor of God daily.

To do: Read Hebrews 4
   Repeat the memory verse several times today and repeat the first 20 weeks memory verses

Smile for the day: COUNTERFEITERS: Workers who put together kitchen cabinets

Week 21 Day 6 Review your memory verse. Record thoughts from this week's devotions and / or prayer requests.

_____
_____
_____
_____
_____
_____
_____
_____
_____
_____
_____
_____
_____
_____
_____
_____
_____
_____
_____
_____
_____
_____
_____
_____
_____
_____
_____
_____

Week 21 Day 7 Review your memory verse. When we pray our prayers should include thanksgiving. Record here what you are thankful for today. Philippians 4:6 "Be anxious for nothing, but in everything by prayer and supplication with thanksgiving let your requests be made known to God."

_____

_____

_____

_____

_____

_____

_____

_____

_____

_____

_____

_____

_____

_____

_____

_____

_____

_____

_____

_____

_____

_____

_____

_____

<u>REVENGE</u>

Vengenance is defined as revenge. And, revenge is a desire to pay injury for injury. Have you ever in your mind thought about doing that? You get an agitated feeling and you're not smiling. And, you're hurting yourself by letting that injury fester inside of you. You're not hurting the other person at all. Let it go; if for no other resaon then to cleanse your thoughts and get peace on the matter. And, turn it over to God. The promise above says He will take care of it.

Romans 12 is about living the Christian life. Verse 2 says, "And do not be conformed to this world, but be transformed by the renewing of your mind, so that you may prove what the will of God is, that which is good and acceptable and perfect." So, to get vengenance out of your mind, you need to choose to renew your mind. Renew is to begin again, to make new again. It's like a mind rewind.

To do: Read Romans 12

Repeat the memory verse several times today and repeat the first 21 weeks memory verses

Smile for the day: Relief: What trees do in the spring

Week 22 Day 2 <u>Memory verse:</u> "Vengenance is mine, I WILL repay. Never take your own vengenance." Romans 12:19

<u>EVIL</u>

Proverbs 20:22 says, "Do not say, I will repay evil. Wait for the Lord and He will save you." Evil is defined as bad, wicked, wrong. No positive words there. In Matthew 5:38-39, Jesus says, "You've heard it said an eye for an eye and a tooth for a tooth. But I say to you, do not resist an evil person; but whoever slaps you on your right cheek, turn the other to him also." That's when you want to say, "really God?" But, remember all of this falls in line with the Second Commandment to love your neighbor as yourself.

Proverbs 24:20 says, "For there will be no future for the evil man; the lamp of the wicked will be put out." John 3:20 says, "For everyone who does evil hates the Light, and does not come to the Light." The Light is Jesus. Proverbs 6:18 tells us that "a heart that devises wicked plans, feet that run rapidly to evil" is one of six things that the Lord hates.

To do: Read Proverbs 6

Repeat the memory verse several times today and repeat the first 21 weeks memory verses

Smile for the day: LEFTBANK: What the robber did when his bag was full of money

Week 22 Day 3 <u>Memory verse:</u> "Vengenance is mine, I WILL repay. Never take your own revenge." Romans 12:19

<u>HONOR</u>

Exodus 20 gives us the ten commandments that were given to Moses. Only one of those commandments has a promise. Verse 12 says, " Honor your father and your mother, that your days may be prolonged in the land which the Lord your God gives you." But, this commandment also has a dire warning. Exodus 21:17 says, "He who curses his father or his mother shall surely be put to death." This is repeated in the New Testament. Matthew 15:4 says: "For God said, honor your father and mother, and He who speaks evil of father or mother is to be put to death."

Life is so short. We are only a breath in the span of eternity. We have friends and family members where parents and children haven't spoken for years. To me that's a trajedy. Your family members are a blessing from the Lord. He chose your parents and He chose your children especially for you. Look carefully at the wording in Mark 10:19: "Do not murder, do not commit adultery, do not steal, do not bear false witness, do not defraud, honor your father and mother." The word honor is used in the commandment about father and mother. Honor is to respect. There are unusual circumstances where there has been abuse. Turn these situation over to the Lord and He will guide you in your responses; physically, spiritually, mentally and emotionally.

To do: Read Matthew 15

Repeat the memory verse several times today and repeat the first 21 weeks memory verses

Smile for the day: PARASITES: What you see from the top of the Eiffel Tower

Week 22 Day 4 <u>Memory verse:</u> "Vengenance is mine, I WILL repay. Never take your own revenge." Romans 12:19

<u>NEVER</u>

When the Lord says "vengenance is mine" what is He saying to us? To me, He's saying He chooses to protect me for my good, for my well being and to lead me in the path of righteousness. He is God. If He chooses to take revenge and tells us not to, then that's what we are to do. Here are some verses that support His promise of I will repay: Deuteronomy 32:35 says, " Vengenance is Mine, and retribution;" Nahum 1:1 says, " A jealous and avenging God is the Lord; the Lord is avenging and wrathful. The Lord takes vengenace on His adversaries, and He reserves wrath for His enemies."

Remember, in the Old Testament, all the stories of Kings and leaders who prayed about going to warfare ahead of time and the Lord promised He would give their enemies into their hands? One of my favorites is Joshua and the battle of Jericho. (Joshua 6). Remember, the Lord tells Joshua in verse 2, "See, I have given Jericho into your hand, with its king and the valiant warriors." Joshua and his men were to march around the city six days and march around the city seven times on the seventh day and then the priests made a long blast on the trumpets and the walls of Jericho fell down. Love that story.

To do: Read Joshua 6

Repeat the memory verse several times today and repeat the first 21 weeks memory verses

Smile for the day: RUBBERNECK: What you do to relax your wife

Week 22 Day 5 <u>Memory verse:</u> "Vengenance is mine, I WILL repay. Never take your own revenge." Romans 12:19

<u>CLEAN HANDS</u>

David fully understood that vengenance belonged to God. Perhaps the greatest story in the Bible about David not taking his own revenge is found in I Saumel 24. This is the story of how David reacted in a situation where he could have taken his own revenge. Here David is speaking to Saul. "Behold, this day your eyes have seen that the Lord has given you today into my hand in the cave, and some said to kill you, but my eye had pity on you; and I said, I will not stretch out my hand against my lord, for he is the Lord's anointed. Indeed, see the edge of your robe in my hand! For in that I cut off the edge of your robe and did not kill you, know and perceive that there is no evil or rebellion in my hands." (verse 10-11) And, in verse 12 David continues with, " May the Lord judge between you and me, and may the Lord avenge me on you; but my hand shall not be against you."

And, in I Samuel 25:39 where David does not kill Nabal, he says in verse 39: "Blessed be the Lord, who has pleaded the cause of my reproach from the hand of Nabal and has kept back His servant from evil. The Lord has also returned the evildoing of Nabal on his own head."

To do: Read I Samuel 24

Repeat the memory verse several times today and repeat the first 21 weeks memory verses

Week 22 Day 6 Review your memory verse. Record thoughts from this week's devotions and / or prayer requests.

_____
_____
_____
_____
_____
_____
_____
_____
_____
_____
_____
_____
_____
_____
_____
_____
_____
_____
_____
_____
_____
_____
_____
_____
_____
_____
_____
_____
_____
_____

Week 22 Day 7 Review your memory verse. When we pray our prayers should include thanksgiving. Record here what you are thankful for today. Philippians 4:6 "Be anxious for nothing, but in everything by prayer and supplication with thanksgiving let your requests be made known to God."

_____

_____

_____

_____

_____

_____

_____

_____

_____

_____

_____

_____

_____

_____

_____

_____

_____

_____

_____

_____

_____

_____

_____

Week 23 Day 1 <u>Memory verse:</u> "Where is the man who fears the Lord? God WILL teach him how to choose the best." Psalm 25:12

<u>AWE</u>

What is the fear of the Lord? To fear the Lord is to hold him in awe, to revere Him for His power and majesty. This healthy kind of fear for the Lord makes us open to respect and revere His word. Proverbs 2:1-5 says, "My son, if you will receive My words and treasure My commandments within you, make your ear attentive to wisdom, incline your heart to understanding; for if you cry for discernment, lift your voice for understanding; if you seek her as silver and search for her as for hidden treasures, then you will discern the fear of the Lord and discover the knowledge of God." Solomon says, "the fear of the Lord is the beginning of wisdom and the knowledge of the Holy One is understanding." (Proverbs 9:10)

When you have an awesome respect for the Lord, this prayer in Psalm 25:5 might be your prayer: "Make me know your ways, O Lord; teach me Your paths. Lead me in Your truth and teach me, for You are the God of my salvation; for You I wait all the day."

To do: Read Psalm 25
Repeat the memory verse several times today and repeat the first 22 weeks memory verses

Smile for the day: SELFISH: What the owner of a seafood store does

<u>Memory verse:</u> **"Where is the man who fears the Lord? God WILL teach him how to choose the best." Psalm 25:12**

BENEFITS

Psalm 25 goes on to list what happens to the person who fears the Lord in addition to (1) teaching him how to choose the best. (2) "His soul will abide in prosperity." (verse 13) (3) "He will make them know His covenant." (verse 14) (4) "The secret of the Lord is for those who fear Him." (verse 14) These are just a few.

Proverbs 14:26,27 says, " In the fear of the Lord there is strong confidence" and "the fear of the Lord is a fountain of Life." Verse 14:2 says, "He who walks in his uprightness fears the Lord." And, Proverbs 19:23 says, "The fear of the Lord leads to life, so that one may sleep satisfied, untouched by evil." Proverbs 14 has much to say regarding the wise versus the foolish.

To do: Read Proverbs 14

Repeat the memory verse several times today and repeat the first 22 weeks memory verses

Smile for the day: POLARIZE: What penguins see with

Week 23 Day 3 <u>Memory verse:</u> "Where is the man who fears the
Lord? God WILL teach him how
to choose the best." Psalm 25:12

<u>EVIL WARNING</u>

In addition to the positives the fear of the Lord can bring to us, there are some negatives that can come to us without the fear of the Lord. Proverbs 8:13a says, "The fear of the Lord is to hate evil" Proverbs 3:7 says, "Do not be wise in your own eyes; fear the Lord and turn away from evil." Why is this important? Because Proverbs 16:5 says, " Everyone who is proud in heart is an abomination to the Lord." Proverbs 15:9 says the same but adds something more saying." The way of the wicked is an abomination to the Lord, but He loves one who pursues righteousness." And Proverbs 14:16 says, "A wise man is cautious and turns away from evil."

In Exodus 20 when God is giving the 10 commandments to the people, there was "thunder and lightning flashes and the sound of the trumpet and the mountain smoking." And when the people saw it, they trembled and stood at a distance and asked Moses to speak himself and they would listen. Moses said in verse 20, "Do not be afraid; for God has come in order to test you, and in order that the fear of Him may remain with you, so that you may not sin."

To do: Read Proverbs 15
Repeat the memory verse several times today and repeat the first 22 weeks memory verses

Smile for the day: EYEDROPPER: A clumsy ophthalmologist

Week 23 Day 4 <u>Memory verse:</u> "Where is the man who fears the Lord? God WILL teach him how to choose the best." Psalm 25:12

<u>GROWING</u>

Proverbs 2:1-5, from Day 1 of this week, spoke of receiving God's words, treasuring His commandments, being attentive to wisdom, inclining our hearts to understanding, crying for discernment. And, by all of these, we discover the knowledge of God. This is now the 23rd week of memorizing promises and reading various chapters from the Bible that relate to those promises. On Day 5, tomorrow, we will be reviewing chapters that we've read about how God teaches us to choose the best.

Proverbs 2 is all about pursuing the fear of the Lord and growing in wisdom, understanding and knowledge. Proverbs 2:6 says, "For the Lord gives wisdom; from His mouth come knowledge and understanding." Proverbs 2:8-9 says, "He preserves the way of His godly ones; you will discern righteousness and justice." If you want more wisdom then ask for it. James 1:5 says, "But if any of you lack wisdom, let him ask of God, who gives to all generously and without reproach, and it will be given to him."

To do: Read Proverbs 2
        Repeat the memory verse several times today and repeat the first 22 weeks memory verses

Smile for the day: BERNADETTE: The act of torching a mortgage

Week 23 Day 5 <u>Memory verse:</u> "Where is the man who fears the Lord? God WILL teach him how to choose the best." Psalm 25:12

REVIEW

Here are some chapters from the Bible to review on various things that God is teaching us on how to choose the best:

1. On <u>wisdom</u>, Review Proverbs 8 and any of the other Proverbs chapters we've read
2. On handling <u>temptation</u> – Review Matthew 4
3. On things to <u>dwell upon</u> – Review Philippians 4
4. On understanding and pursuing <u>love</u> – Review I John 4 and I Corinthians 13
5. On <u>how to treat others</u> – Review Matthew 7, James 5, Romans 14
6. On instructions regarding <u>righteousness</u> – Review Psalm 37, Colossians 3, Luke 6
7. On <u>living the Christian life</u> – Review Romans 12
8. On the power of <u>the tongue</u> and <u>what to say</u> – Review Matthew 15, James 1, James 3
9. On <u>working out your salvation</u> – Review Philippians 2
10. On <u>standing firm, having discipline & endurance</u> – Review Hebrews 12, Phil 1, Ephesians 6

Psalm 32:8 says, "I WILL instruct you and teach you in the way you should go; I WILL counsel you with My eye upon you." Here are three more promises. How are you doing in choosing the best? Hopefully, this is a daily goal we all have.

To do: Week 24 has no memory verse. Suggested reading: Review daily one or two of the chapters above for next week. Repeat all 23 weeks memory verses

Week 23 Day 6 Review your memory verse. Record thoughts from this week's devotions and / or prayer requests.

_____

_____

_____

_____

_____

_____

_____

_____

_____

_____

_____

_____

_____

_____

_____

_____

_____

_____

_____

_____

_____

_____

_____

_____

_____

_____

_____

Week 23 Day 7 Review your memory verse. When we pray our prayers should include thanksgiving. Record here what you are thankful for today. Philippians 4:6 "Be anxious for nothing, but in everything by prayer and supplication with thanksgiving let your requests be made known to God."

_____

_____

_____

_____

_____

_____

_____

_____

_____

_____

_____

_____

_____

_____

_____

_____

_____

_____

_____

_____

_____

_____

_____

_____

_____

Week 24 NO MEMORY VERSE TOPIC: X-IT SIN

What Is Sin?

There is no memory verse this week. The topic is SIN and how do we **X-IT** from SIN

(1) First of all, what is sin? Sin is first of all separation from God. Sin is transgression. Transgression is a violation of a command. Sin is lawlessness. I John 3:4 says, "Everyone who practices sin also practices lawlessness; and sin is lawlessness." I John 5:17a says, "All unrighteousness is sin."

(2) Second, what are the sins of lawlessnes specifically? "Therefore, consider the members of your body as dead to immorality, impurity, passion, evil desire, and greed, which amounts to idolatry. For it is because of these things that the wrath of God will come upon the sons of disobedience." (Colossians 3:5-6) And, Galations 5:19-21 says, "Now the deeds of the flesh are evident, which are: idolatry, sorcery, enmities, strife, jealousy, outbursts of anger, disputes, dissentions, factions, envying, drunkenness, carousing."

Jesus Died For Our Sins

(1) Third, What did Jesus do for our sins? "And He Himself bore our sins in His body on the cross, so that we might die to sin and live in righteousness; for by His wounds you were healed." (I Peter 2:24) "You know that He appeared in order to take away sins; and in Him there is no sin." (I John 3:5)

(2) Fourth, Why did Jesus die for our sins? "He made Him who knew no sin to be sin on our behalf, so that we might become the righteousness of God in Him." (II Corinthians 5:21)

KAY BRYANT

We Need To Confess Our Sins

(1) Fifth, <u>We need to confess our</u> sins. Paul says in Acts 22:16, " Get up and be baptized, and wash away your sins, calling on His name." Peter says in Acts 2:38, "Repent, and each of you be baptized in the name of Jesus Christ for the forgiveness of your sins; and you will receive the gift of the Holy Spirit,"

(2) Sixth, <u>All have sinned.</u> "For all have sinned and fall short of the glory of God." (Romans 3:23)

(3) Seventh, <u>what happens when you confess?</u> "He who conceals his transgressions will not prosper, but he who confesses and forsakes them will find compassion." (Proverbs 28:13)

Resisting Sin

(1) Eighth, <u>how do we resist sin?</u> "Submit to God. Resist the devil and he will flee from you." (James 4:7) "But I say, walk by the Spirit, and you will not carry out the desire of the flesh." (Galations 5:16)

(2) Ninth, <u>God will help us.</u> "No temptation has overtaken you but such as is common to man and God is faithful, who will not allow you to be tempted beyond what you are able, but with the temptation will provide the way of escape also, so that you will be able to endure it." (Ist Corinthians 10:13)

To do: Repeat the first 23 weeks of memory verses every day this week

Week 25 Day 1 Memory verse: "You WILL know the truth and the truth WILL make you free." John 8:32

THE SOURCE

Truth is genuineness and honesty. God knows all things, so we can trust anything He says as the truth. He determines the truth because He is the source of truth Himself. The verse right before John 8:32 says, "if you continue in My word, then you are truly disciples of Mine." (verse 31) John 1:14 says, "And the Word became flesh, and dwelt among us, and we saw His glory, glory as of the only begotten from the Father, full of grace and truth." So, one way we are going to find the truth is in the scriptures.

Jesus confirms what is said in John 1:14 in John 14:6, "I am the way, and the truth, and the life; no one comes to the Father but through Me." Psalm 119:160 says, "The sum of Your word is truth." The more we know about Jesus, the more we know the truth.

To do: Read John 8

Repeat the memory verse several times today & repeat the 23 previous weeks memory verses

Smile for the day: At a car dealership: "The best way to get back on your feet – miss a car payment.

Week 25 Day 2 <u>Memory verse:</u> "You WILL know the truth and the truth WILL make you free." John 8:32

THE HELPER

For the New Testament Christians and Christians today, one way God makes His truth known is through the Holy Spirit. The Holy Spirit is also referred to as the Spirit of Truth. John 16:13-15 says, "But when He, the Spirit of Truth comes, He will guide you into all the truth; for He will not speak on His own iniative, but whatever He hears, He will speak; and He will disclose to you what is to come. He will glorify Me, for He will take of Mine and will disclose it to you. All things that the Father has are mine; therefore I said that He takes of Mine and will disclose it to you." I hope you picked up on all the "wills" in those verses – promises for you. So, again, we need to spend time in the Bible faithfully and regularly for the Holy Spirit to show us the truths of the scripture.

John 14:17 refers to the Helper as "the Spirit of Truth, whom the world cannot receive, because it does not see Him or know Him, but you know Him because He abides with you and will be in you."

To do: Read John 16

Repeat the memory verse several times today & repeat the 23 previous weeks memory verses

Smile for the day: Another sign on septic tank truck: "Caution – this truck is full of political promises"

<u>WORD OF TRUTH</u>

What is the word of truth? Ephesians 1:13 says, " In Him, you also, after listening to the <u>message of truth</u>, the gospel of your salvation – having also believed, you were sealed in Him with the Holy Spirit of promise." And this is reinforced in Colossians 1:5 where Paul is giving thanks and praying for the faithful saints at Colossae: " Because of the hope laid up for you in heaven, of which you previously heard in the <u>word of truth</u>, the gospel." So, the word of truth is the gospel.

And, we have a responsibility on how we handle the word of truth. II Timothy 2:15 says, " Be diligent to present yourself approved to God as a workman who does not need to be ashamed, accurately handling the <u>word of truth."</u> James 1:18 says, "In the exercise of His will He brought us forth by the <u>word of truth,</u> so that we would be a kind of first fruits among His creatures." How we handle the word of truth, both in word and action, is our witness to the unsaved.

To do: Read Ephesians 1

Repeat the memory verse several times today and repeat the 23 weeks of memory verses

Smile for the day: What did the man say when the bridge fell on him? The suspension is killing me

Week 25 Day 4 <u>Memory verse:</u> "You WILL know the truth and the truth WILL make you free." John 8:32

SET APART

In John 17:17 Jesus is praying to the Father for His disciples saying," sanctify them in the truth; Your word is the truth." We are also God's disciples and so He's saying this prayer for us as well. Sanctify means to set apart as for God's special use and purpose. Sanctification is an on-going process to holiness throughout the Christian's life. We are to be set apart in the truth which is another reason to be in the word on a daily basis. This is how we become absorbed with the truth.

As we become grounded in the truths presented in scripture, we develop convictions on how to think, act, feel, etc. Have you ever met someone who told you they do not sin? They say this because they believe they haven't broken any of the 10 commandments and therefore they have no sin. I John 1:8 says, "If we say that we have no sin, we are deceiving ourselves and the truth is not in us." I John 2:4 says, "The one who says, 'I have come to know Him,' and does not keep His commandments, is a liar, and the truth is not in him."

To do: Read John 17
        Repeat the memory verse several times today and repeat the 23 weeks of memory verses

Smile for the day: On a maternity room door: "Push. Push. Push."

Week 25 Day 5 <u>Memory verse:</u> "You WILL know the truth and the truth WILL make you free." John 8:32

<u>FREEDOM</u>

What will the truth make us free from? Romans 6 talks about how we were slaves to sin before becoming a Christian and then we became obedient from the heart "and having been freed from sin, you became slaves of righteousness." (verses 17,18) Romans 8:2 says, "For the law of the Spirit of life in Christ Jesus has set you free from the law of sin and death." Once again, we need to be in the word to become obedient from the heart. The more we learn about God's truth, the freer we become.

What are we to do with our freedom? Galations 5:13 says, "For you were called to freedom, brethren; only do not turn your freedom into an opportunity for the flesh, but through love serve one another." Paul says in I Corinthians 9:19, "For though I am free from all men, I have made myself a slave to all, so that I may win more." Wow! He sure set a standard for us. Ephesians 4:15 says, "but speaking the truth in love, we are to grow up in all aspects into Him who is the head, even Christ."

To do: Read Romans 6

Repeat the memory verse several times today and repeat the 23 weeks of memory verses

Smile for the day: In a restaurant window: "Don't stand there & be hungry; come on in & get fed up."

Week 25 Day 6 Review your memory verse. Record thoughts from this week's devotions and / or prayer requests.

_____

_____

_____

_____

_____

_____

_____

_____

_____

_____

_____

_____

_____

_____

_____

_____

_____

_____

_____

_____

_____

_____

_____

_____

_____

_____

_____

_____

_____

Week 25 Day 7 Review your memory verse. When we pray our prayers should include thanksgiving. Record here what you are thankful for today. Philippians 4:6 "Be anxious for nothing, but in everything by prayer and supplication with thanksgiving let your requests be made known to God."

_____
_____
_____
_____
_____
_____
_____
_____
_____
_____
_____
_____
_____
_____
_____
_____
_____
_____
_____
_____
_____
_____
_____
_____
_____

KAY BRYANT

Week 26 <u>ZEAL</u>: Having an eagerness in pursuit of the Lord - Our goal.

Here we are at the end of our 26 weeks. By now, you have committed 24 promises of God to memory, 25 if you've memorized John 3:16. You have also been enriched by the words of scripture in regards to these promises. So, now we are to the goal of all of this memorizing and learning: to have a zeal for the Lord. Zeal is fervor, passion, intense feeling. Zeal comes from the Greek word zelos which is defined as ardor or fervor of spirit.

<u>ZEAL OF THE LORD</u>

II Kings 19:31 says, "For out of Jerusalem will go forth a remnant, and out of Mount Zion survivors. The zeal of the Lord will perform this." Isaiah 9:7 says, "There will be no end to the increase of His government or of peace, on the throne of David and over his kingdom, to establish it and to uphold it with justice and righteousness from then on and forevermore. The zeal of the Lord of hosts will accomplish this." The Lord of hosts is a God of compassion and mercy and love. Revelation 3:19 says, "Those whom I love, I reprove and disciplne; therefore, be zealous and repent."

Joel 2 is all about returning to the Lord with all your heart. Joel 2:18 says, "Then the Lord will be zealous for His land and will have pity on His people."

<u>JESUS ZEAL</u>

Remember in John 2:14-17 when Jesus turns over the tables of those doing business in the temple? And He said, "zeal for Your house will consume me" He had righteous indignation at what was happpening in His Father's house. Remember in Matthew 4 where Jesus is being tempted by the devil? Even though he's hungry after having fasted 40 days and 40 nights, His zeal for the Lord results in His striving against the devil after being tempted 3 times. In all 3 situations, He fires back to the devil <u>words of scripture. I</u>n verse 4 He says, " Man shall not live on bread alone, but on every word that proceeds out of the mouth of God." In verse 7 He says, "You shall not put the Lord your God to the test." In verse 10 He says, " You shall worship the Lord your God, and serve Him only."

<u>WHAT ARE WE TO HAVE A ZEAL FOR</u>

Zeal is a word applied anywhere someone has a passion for something or someone. Think of the Olympic participants and the zeal they have for their sport. Their zeal results in countless hours of practicing, resulting in many sacrifices in other areas, a total commitment, and eagerness about what they are doing. We are to pursue our faith and our Christian walk as if we are preparing for the Olympics. We are to have a zeal for the faith, to be passionate about His word, eager to learn and grow and share His word with others. David is a great example of his zeal for the Lord. He says in Isaish 26:8-9b: "Your name, even Your memory, <u>is the desire of our souls. A</u>t night <u>my soul longs for You,</u> indeed, <u>my spirit within me seeks you diligently.</u>" Let David's zeal be an example for us.

My prayer is that you will grow in your relationship with the Lord; that your trust and your faith will be contiually growing and, as you memorize more scriptures, you will be confident, prepared and encouraged for the life that we are asked to live.

To do: Repeat all the memory verses you have learned in this book

Promise Memory Verses Alphabetically

A – As for me, I <u>WILL</u> call upon the Lord; and the Lord <u>SHALL</u> save me (Psalm 55:16)

B – But the Lord is faithful & <u>WILL</u> strengthen & protect you from the evil one (II Thess 3:3)

C - Call to me, and I <u>WILL</u> answer you & I <u>WILL</u> tell you great things which you do not know (Jeremiah 33:3)

D – Draw near unto God & He <u>WILL</u> draw near to you (James 4:8)

E – Everyone who shall confess me before men, I WILL also confess him before my Father (Matthew 10:32)

F- Follow Me and I <u>WILL</u> make you fishers of men (Matthew 4:19)

G – God <u>WILL</u> fill your mouth with laughter, and your lips with shouting.(Job 8:21)

H – He <u>WILL</u> wipe away every tear from their eyes; no longer any death, mourning, crying or pain (Revelation 21:4)

I – If you keep my commandments, you <u>WILL</u> abide in my love. (John 15:10)

J – Jesus said, Judge not so that you <u>WILL</u> not be judged (Matt 7:1)

K – Know that I <u>WILL</u> pour out my Spirit on you. I <u>WILL</u> make My word known to you. (Proverbs 1:23)

L – Let us not lose heart in doing good, for in due time we <u>WILL</u> reap if we don't grow weary (Galations 6:9)

M – My presence <u>SHALL</u> go with you, & I <u>WILL</u> give you rest (Exodus 33:14)

N – Nor height, depth, nor any created thing, <u>WILL</u> be able to separate us from the love of God (Romans 8:39)

O – Only believe, that He who began a good work in you <u>WILL</u> perfect it until the day of Jesus Christ. (Phil 1:6)

P – Peace I leave with you; My peace <u>I GIVE</u> to you; not as the world gives do <u>I GIVE</u> to you. (John 14:27)

Q – Quick to hear, slow to speak & slow to anger for this is God"s <u>WILL</u>. (James 1:19)

R – Remain faithful until death & I <u>WILL</u> give you the crown of life (Rev 2:10)

S – Surely I <u>WILL</u> help you. Surely I <u>WILL</u> uphhold you with my rigtheous right hand. (Isaiah 41:10bc)

T – The free gift God <u>WILL</u> give is eternal life in Christ Jesus our Lord. (Romans 6:23)

U – Use the full armor of God so that you <u>WILL</u> be able to stand firm against the devil's schemes. (Ephesians 6:11)

V – Vengenance is mine, I <u>WILL</u> repay. Never take your own revenge (Romans 12:19)

W – Where is the man who fears the Lord? God <u>WILL</u> teach him how to choose the best (Psalm 25:12)

X – X it sin

Y – You <u>WILL</u> know the truth, and the truth <u>WILL</u> make you free. (John 8:32)

Z – Zeal – having an eagerness in pursuit of the Lord

CPSIA information can be obtained
at www.ICGtesting.com
Printed in the USA
FSHW011320130920
73715FS